Advance Praise

"Working across multiple genres and many decades of what he calls "bad prison films," Dr. Benjamin Boyce's *The Spectacle of Punishment* chronicles how such media is saturated with casual racism, scenes of carnage, institutional violence masquerading as comedy, and an unquestioned commitment to law-and-order not as the search for justice, but as a machine of retribution."

— Stephen J. Hartnett, PhD., author of *Democratic Dissent & the Cultural Fictions of Antebellum America, Executing Democracy* vol. 1 & vol. 2 and *Incarceration Nation;* editor of *Captured Words/ Free Thoughts* vol. 1-19, *Working for Justice: A Handbook of Prison Education and Activism,* and *Challenging the Prison-Industrial Complex: Activism, Arts & Educational Alternatives*

"Dr. Ben Boyce calls out what folks outside prison easily take to be natural and normal. The outlaw seeking redemption struggling against the lone unethical prison authority, scenes of a "lawless" place where incarcerated folks abuse each other—Ben reveals them as not only false, but also harmful, masking a $300 billion a year system that warehouses people rather than rehabilitates them."

— Christina Foust, PhD., author of *Meditations on Immediate Resistance, Aesthetics as Weapons in the 'War of Ideas:' Exploring the Digital and Typographic in American Conservative Web Sites,* and *A Return to Feminine Public Virtue: Judge Judy and the Myth of the Tough Mother.*

"While media scholars and cultural critics have written extensively about media representations of crime, the area of the criminal [in]justice system that has received the least attention is mass incarceration in the prison industrial complex. In recent years this is beginning to change, and

Benjamin Boyce's *The Spectacle of Punishment* is one of the newest, and one of the best, books to take on the relationship between media and the deeply misleading notions about incarceration that have warped public opinion about prisons and prisoners for decades.

Uniquely suited to write about media and incarceration because of his own experiences as both a former prisoner and a prison educator, and now a communication professor, Boyce successfully integrates scholarly sources, a wealth of examples from prison films and television shows, and his own story, into a compelling analysis of the central narratives and images of prison-based media and how they must be challenged if the current dysfunctional and cruel system is ever to be transformed into something more effective and humane.

Boyce argues that prison films and television shows are divided up into three broad and overlapping rhetorical frames that he identifies as: prison as playground, prison as penance, and prison as paradox. He then provides numerous examples of each, along with careful analysis and smart insights into the ways that these frames may influence viewers' imaginations about mass incarceration, and the forgotten real people that are forced to live behind prison walls.

Along the way he draws on an impressive range of literature by important thinkers like Plato, Wilde, Freud, Jung, Arendt, the Frankfurt School, Burke, Foucault, de Certeau, and hooks, alongside many communication and media scholars who have written about the prison industrial complex. His final chapters delve into his own experiences, where he offers important insights into the tragedy of the current system, and proposals of changes that are necessary if we are ever to break the seemingly endless cycle of neglect, fear, retribution, and punishment."

— Dr. Bill Yousman, Graduate Program in Media Literacy and Digital Culture at Sacred Heart University

THE SPECTACLE
OF PUNISHMENT

THE SPECTACLE OF PUNISHMENT

*Lessons from a
Century of Prison Films*

Benjamin Boyce, PhD

Apprentice
House Press
Loyola University Maryland

First Edition

Hardcover ISBN: 978-1-62720-428-6
Paperback ISBN: 978-1-62720-429-3
Ebook ISBN: 978-1-62720-430-9

Design by Erin Hurley
Editorial Development by Sam Dickson

Published by Apprentice House Press

Apprentice
House Press
Loyola University Maryland

Loyola University Maryland
4501 N. Charles Street, Baltimore, MD 21210
410.617.5265
www.ApprenticeHouse.com
info@ApprenticeHouse.com

Dedicated to bell hooks for teaching us how to love.

Contents

Author's Note

I begin with a full confession. I'm an outlaw, or at least I was at one point. In the eyes of many, that means I always will be. Once convicted, citizens of the United States enter a parallel world which Michelle Alexander rightly describes as "permanent second-class status . . . the New Jim Crow."[1] For the rest of our lives we will be judged by strangers for the worst things we have ever done. We are obliged to confess on demand, and to beg eternally for forgiveness and redemption. Once incarcerated, our debt to society is never fully paid.

In late Summer of 2004, I was arrested for a string of petty thefts committed to feed an addiction to heroin, fentanyl and cocaine. After a series of court appearances, I became Michigan Department of Corrections Inmate 470236. My sentence began in the largest walled prison on earth, a fortress in Jackson, Michigan built in the early 1900s to house in influx of new captives to the war on drugs. For a long time, I thought that "criminal" and "addicted person" would forever remain my most salient identities. Then, in 2018, I finished my PhD, making me a Doctor of Communication. Yet decades after my release from prison and years after my certification, I am still regularly confronted with the mistakes of my youth and forced to explain anew decisions I made on the worst days of my life.

Language is infused with power. Our labels and titles impact our ability to succeed. I've been to prison twice during my life, once incarcerated, and later as an instructor for in-prison college classes. I was treated differently based on my label at the time, "teacher" versus "inmate." Our labels can make us or break us, but seldom do we have much of a choice in which we wind up carrying around. Words like prisoner, inmate, convict and offender flatten the identity of those who find themselves labeled. Person-based language is always preferable when discussing real humans, because seldom are our reductions reflective of who we really are. To that end, I avoid the use of flattening labels, recognizing that language can build people up just as easily as it can tear them down.

What's the difference between an inmate and an incarcerated person? An inmate is just an inmate, while an incarcerated person is most definitely many other things which we may still discover. When I do use terms like "outlaw," "lawman," "inmate" or "monster" in this book, I use them in reference to the characters conjured up by producers and writers, not as subjective descriptions of the people or stories being discussed. Those in prison are not responsible for the stereotypes pedaled by Hollywood. Movies and television shows are capitalistic productions created to produce profit. I hold creators accountable for their products, and so do you. That's how capitalism works.

My goal isn't to bring down Hollywood or ruin your favorite movies. I'm hoping to force the hands of producers, and to incentivize a deliberate move toward more humanizing representations of *all* oppressed groups, including incarcerated people. I wish to entice, not threaten. Blockbusters that gross tens-of-millions on opening weekend and those that flop are differentiated by just one thing—how many people pay to see them. As the media landscape of the twenty-first century continues to take shape, we appear to be entering an age of empowerment where amplification of one's voice is easier than ever before. Let's work to make it an age where misleading or oppressive representations are less popular than those that lift up and tell the whole story.

Introduction

Why Media Matters

"Stereotypes tend to be both self-fulfilling and self-perpetuating precisely because they help us to explain the world."[2] —*Travis Dixon*

"Allegories and myths are ways that societies keep track of their contradictions . . . new ones are constructed as required."[3] —*Laura Kipnis*

The media we consume teaches us about the world, whether we realize it or not. This axiom is more important now than ever before, for the further we have proceeded into this human experiment called civilization, the larger the machine of propaganda has grown. Of course, media isn't inherently evil. Your nightly dose of *CSI* or *Law and Order* doesn't make you a bad person. It just makes you susceptible to the effects of unchallenged messages received via media representation. Unless you recognize what is being communicated and actively resist the messages offered, you will find your base programming updated as you learn things about the world.

The explosion of mass mediated images in the early twentieth century paved the way for a field of research known as cultural criticism.[4] One of the most popular iterations of cultural criticism explores media and its ability to make us believe things that aren't entirely true. We've all had this experience. You might have looked for the escape hatch in an elevator—the one you have seen in dozens of movies, but in real life it's not there. You have probably heard movie cops yell, "Cover me!" before charging into the line of fire, or you've watched them steal a car from a citizen while in hot pursuit of a suspect. It happens so often on television that these things feel typical. Movie heroes wounded by bullets keep going like it is no big deal. Those same bullets blow other characters backward when they are shot. Cars jump, crash, or even fly through buildings then keep driving. It's all complete nonsense, but we unknowingly come to believe a lot of it anyway. That's the magic of media.

By the 1940s, Theodor Adorno and Max Horkheimer were already lamenting our social habits of "aesthetic mass consumption," including our love of media spectacles designed to appeal to a mass audience.[5] Walter Benjamin diagnosed us as having an unhealthy attraction to the "phony spell of commodity" before most homes contained a television.[6] In the 1980s, Michel de Certeau recognized the ways in which media teach us things even when we know they're probably not true:

> "the spectator-observer *knows* that they are merely 'semblances,' the results of manipulations—'*I know perfectly well that it's so much hogwash*'—*but all the same,* he assumes that these simulations have the status of the real."[7]

Building on these foundations, a host of media critics have now proposed theories to help us understand how we come to learn things from our television, movies and smartphone screens. As the barrage of media productions has continued relatively unchecked, we have established a growing bag of tools for diagnosing and identifying the worst of media manipulations. Cultural critic bell hooks has shown how media representations of poverty teach viewers, wrongly, that the poor are immoral and driven by greed, and that wealth typically springs from ethical behavior.[8] Naturally, those who watch a lot of television and film come to believe that wealth is usually earned through hard work, that most poor people are largely responsible for their own plight, and that most wealthy people are good-hearted philanthropists who spend their lives seeking out poor people worthy of assistance. The regular consumption of these stories naturally causes viewers to distrust and even despise those who are struggling with poverty, and to blame them for their own lot in life. As hooks explains:

> "Much of the magic of cinema lies in the medium's power to give us something other than life as is…Movies do not merely offer us the opportunity to reimagine the culture we most intimately know on the screen, they create culture."[9]

That's a powerful accusation, because culture is all we've got when it comes to understanding what the world was like before we got here, and what it will be like after we are gone.

It's more than just our fiction. Television news programs constantly overrepresent the number of crimes committed by nonwhite people and the number of arrests made by white officers, causing viewers to unwittingly accept the false narrative that crime is much more common than it actually is, and that it is usually committed by nonwhite suspects.[10] Media representations of the prison industrial complex rely on gruesome tails of mayhem and murder to keep viewers tuned in, leaving us more supportive of punishment-oriented policies, up to and including the death penalty.[11] Viewers of television crime dramas come to believe that the police are generally successful at reducing crime, that they only use force when necessary, and that even when misconduct or abuse at the hands of police occurs, it seldom leads to false confessions.[12] Even when cinematic prison spaces feature dialogue and plot appearing to challenge the norm of mass incarceration, we often still come to endorse an expanding and harshening correctional system based on the bad behavior of those we see inside.[13] None of these effects take place consciously within the viewer's mind. If you ask television audiences how much their opinions have changed based on their media diet, they usually claim to be uninfluenced by the stories they consume and immune to the messages that affect the rest of us.[14] The human condition is all about self-deception.

Meanwhile, Hollywood appears stuck in a *Matrix* glitch of *Déjà vu*, repeatedly filming the same scenes over and over, convincing us that each is new, fresh, and worthy of our coin. Nine *Spiderman* films were released between 2002 – 2022.[15] Prime time is now packed with redoes of sitcoms that were canceled decades ago: *The Wonder Years, Saved by the Bell, CSI: Las Vegas, Quantum Leap, Sex in the City (...And Just like That), True Blood, Frasier, A League of their Own, Charmed, Will & Grace, (Fresh Prince of) Bel-Air,* and *Gossip Girls,* along with plenty of others. Reboots have become an increasingly popular solution to the nonstop consumer demand for content that appears to be new while still scratching familiar itches. We want the freshness of novelty alongside the comfort of the common.

At the same time, new media streaming services pop up so often that many of us can't remember which we have subscribed to and which we have not. Our television and film options have become more diverse than ever before. We find ourselves in a new era of social media, a world where influencers and media agents are a thing, and where "going viral" with a snarky tweet is often more powerful than a lifetime of research assembled into a well-constructed article. Along with the emergence of new forms of media, we have watched the machine of peer reviewed research explode. There is, it seems, a journal for everything; *Porn Studies, The International Journal of Tourism Sciences,* and even *The Journal of Controversial Ideas* are all well established. It is harder than ever to make one's message stand out from the cacophony of media noise. Productions which rise above the chaos must be louder and sharper than ever before if they are to compete in a market inundated with more content every day.

Media productions reflect our cultural norms, but they are also a reflection *of* cultural norms. They show us the truth about ourselves and how we think, but they also shape our truths and our thoughts. Bell hooks wasn't exaggerating when she claimed that media literally "create culture."[16] Sometimes that's no big deal, like when a film focuses on a topics we already know about from personal experience. But when media representations venture from the mundane into the bizarre, viewers find themselves in unfamiliar territory, consuming information we cannot balance out with real life experience or personal relationships. When it is the only thing available, we come to accept fiction as fact. The prisons in our movies become the prisons in our imaginations, and we often lack the experience necessary to counterbalance the spectacle. As Michelle Brown has suggested, "much of the popular knowledge about punishment is constructed—in spaces far from the social realities and the social facts that define mass incarceration."[17]

As you progress through this book, I invite you to keep in mind the films and television shows you grew up with and were drawn to throughout your life. My focus is the prison environment, but these effects hold true regardless of the subject matter; so long as the topic is a person, place or thing with which we have little or no personal experience, we are prone to be misled by media representations. Remember the things you "learned" which later turned out to be untrue or misleading. Try to draw your own lines backwards to the media that taught you those things, whether they were related to prison, mental health, restricted institutions, a cultural group you didn't have much experience with, a faraway land, or even a war zone. As we shall see, representations of faraway places and off-limits locations do cultural damage by (mis)informing our opinions and our behavior. We unwittingly come to accept that the world resembles the information we soak up from mass mediated spectacles of entertainment.

Chapter 1

The Outlaw and the Lawman in Les Misérables

"What we mean by 'archetype' is in itself irrepresentable, but has effects which make visualization of it possible, namely, the archetypal image and ideas. We meet with a similar situation in physics: there the smallest particles are themselves irrepresentable but have effects from the nature of which we can build up a model. The archetypal image, the motif or mythologem, is a construction of this kind."[18] –Carl Jung

On Christmas morning of 2012, Universal Pictures released the latest in a series of films based on Victor Hugo's 1862 classic outlaw story, *Les Misérables*.[19] It was, once again, a hit, bringing in $283 million during its first month in theaters, earning numerous prize nominations, and eventually winning three Golden Globes and three Academy Awards.[20] The public endorsement was not unusual. Since 1985, *Les Misérables* has been translated into 21 languages, performed in 43 countries, won upwards of 100 awards, and been seen by more than 60 million people.[21] As early as 1909, movie producers were taking advantage of the story's notoriety.[22] And to this day, there is something about this narrative that continues to resonate with audiences across the globe.

Les Misérables has proven longstanding in part because of archetypal characters who have since been repackaged and re-presented in countless other stories. An archetype is a recurring character in literature, film or television, one who is identifiable by commonly held traits despite different names or back stories used to make them appear unique. As Carl Jung explained, "The archetype is a tendency to form such representations as a motif—representations that can vary a great deal in detail without losing their basic pattern."[23] The bumbling sidekick is a recurring archetype; despite different names, costumes, sizes and shapes, this character shows up over and over in hero stories, usually to make the hero's deeds appear more valiant.[24] The cool teacher is an archetype because, despite different grades, classrooms, subjects and students, story after story has employed the dynamic character of the cool educator who stands out from the rest by devoting themselves to their students.[25] The explosive kiss that unlocks the main character from forced slumber is an archetype, whether *Sleeping Beauty, The Wonder Years* or *Free Guy*, because they all follow the same basic storyline.[26] Anytime you think to yourself, "this feels familiar. I bet I know what they are going to do," that's probably the result of living in a culture packed with archetypes.

Archetypes make us feel comfortable because we know what to expect, so once they set up shop in a culture's media representations, they stick around for a long time. As Aniela Jaffe suggests, "The intertwined history of religion and art, reaching back to prehistoric times, is the record that our ancestors have left of the symbols that were meaningful and moving to them."[27] Our archetypes are the shadows of stories which were valued and shared by those who came long before us. That's great news for cultural critics, because it means we can use archetypes to establish genealogical patterns in media which reveal underlying trends in cultural norms. We can decode them to better understand ourselves and our place in the world.

Les Misérables introduced two major archetypal characters, the outlaw desperately seeking redemption and the lawman who refuses to give it to him. Their behaviors have remained consistent for more than 150 years despite clever updates in character identities disguising them as different people in different stories. Their names and histories might change, but their patterns remain the same. Certainly, *Les Misérables* was not the first time these archetypes showed up. They are, in many ways, as old as humankind, and their stories have long been used to pass cultural norms and traditions on through generations. But given both the age and the popularity of *Les Misérables*, it's fair to say it has been responsible for introducing a lot of people to these classic characters. The archetypal outlaw, and his counterpart, the lawman, are a big part of what makes any prison films work. They are the magic ingredients that, when mixed and baked properly, yield reliable results.

Redemption Denied

The protagonist in *Les Misérables* is Jean Valjean, an outlaw who enters the story as a recently paroled, angry social outcast.[28] And who can blame him? Valjean was originally arrested for stealing a loaf of bread to feed his family, and despite his best efforts to move beyond his conviction, the rest of the world appears unwilling to give him a second chance. He carries a set of yellow identification papers marking him as a dangerous criminal, and he struggles to find employment, food, and lodging wherever he goes.[29] As viewers, we feel bad for him, that is, until he is taken in and cared for by a stranger and responds to the good deed by making off with the man's silver in the middle of the night. Viewers, along with those who had turned Valjean away based on his record, seem for a moment to have been correct in their assumptions about his character, as he proves himself to be an incorrigible thief. As the story picks up steam, viewers are invited to wonder whether this outlaw is capable of redemption at all.

Valjean is arrested and returned to the house to answer for his crime, but in a twist, the homeowner claims the items were a gift, and Valjean is subsequently released.[30] The stranger's kindness is a turning point in the story. Valjean the common criminal begins the transformation into Valjean the redeemed outlaw, and as viewers, we find ourselves engrossed in a plot driven by emotions we seldom experience so richly in our own lives: relief, fear, anticipation, terror, and most importantly, redemption. Throughout the following years, Valjean rescues a young girl from a life of abuse, becomes Mayor of a local town, and even saves the life of a stranger who becomes pinned beneath a cart. Redemption becomes his sole mission in life, and as viewers we join his team, rooting for his success as he continues to prove himself through his actions. By the story's end, Valjean is hard to hate, while the lawman who relentlessly chases him has taken on many of the traits which we originally disliked in Valjean.

I am not the first to recognize *Les Misérables* as what Mike Nellis has called "the foundational redemptive text."[31] Nellis tracks the ways Valjean's redemption is established through specific events: he "experiences guilt and takes responsibility for his future, makes amends by becoming a productive citizen and prevents suffering in another generation," while consistently enduring "whatever moral duty requires of him."[32] This basic archetypal character of the outlaw seeking redemption has remained a prominent figure in prison media for more than a century. The level of success which the outlaw experiences in their attempts at reformation varies from story to story. But even when the archetypal outlaw discards the idea of redemption altogether, the desire to make a sincere change always materializes at some point in their story.

Les Misérables also introduced audiences to a second archetypal character, unrelenting Police Inspector Javert, who represents the counterpart of the archetypal outlaw seeking redemption. Javert serves as the story's primary antagonist, chasing the reformed Valjean wherever he flees regardless of the years that pass or the amends Valjean appears to make. As Nellis explains:

> "Javert, embodies all that is hostile to the principle of giving offenders second chances . . . he represents both the long shadow of imprisonment, and the impossibility of ever becoming free of its influence or stigma, and the diffusion of penal authority into every crevice of public life."[33]

Javert simply knows that Valjean is irredeemable, and near the end of the story, when the man he is chasing puts his own safety in peril to save the inspector's life, Javert finds himself unable to accept the outlaw's virtuous deed. Torn between his moral and his official responsibilities, Javert takes his own life. Narratives such as Javert's suicide reveal the inability of the archetypal lawman to recognize a sincere change of heart in the character of the redeemed outlaw. When faced with the reality of a world where outlaws are capable of redemption, the lawman in *Les Misérables* simply can't go on living.

Cops and Robbers on TV

The two archetypes detailed above, the outlaw seeking redemption and the lawman who refuses to give it to him, continue to appear as recurring characters in contemporary television shows and films. Hollywood has only dumped fuel on the fire Hugo lit with *Les Misérables*. The following list is by no means extensive, but I have attempted to select films and television shows that were popular at the time of their release, as evidenced by revenue, awards, star power and critic reviews. My goal is not to prove these characters exist in every prison film. Instead, I am interested in explaining the various ways these archetypes show up, why they often appear to be different characters despite eerie (and often obvious) similarities, and most importantly, how they teach us lessons about the world without us realizing it. If you find that your favorite prison story is not included in this list, pause before you move on to the next chapter and consider how the characters in that story also fit the archetypes outlined below.

Prior to the 1940s, most US homes did not have a television, so our journey begins on the big screen in 1932, with a film called *The Last Mile*.[34] Richard Walters plays the film's redemption-seeking outlaw, a man on death row who continues to profess his innocence as the clock winds down toward his final hours. The film's obstinate lawman is played by a guard who is eventually killed in a botched breakout attempt. But our archetypal outlaw finds his redemption in the end despite being shot while participating in the escape. He awakens in the hospital, having been exonerated of the original crime based on new evidence. Early on in cinema, producers recognized the ability of the prison space to warp viewer expectations, as we are more than willing to forgive Walter's participation in a getaway that resulted in the death of numerous guards and others inside prison once we realize he shouldn't have been there in the first place. Seldom are we so tolerant of bad behavior as when those acts take place in the setting of a cinematic prison. We almost expect the space to warp the judgement and conduct of those inside.

A few years later, Hollywood took a shot at its first of many reboots with a story that is actually older than *Les Misérables*. One of the first film version of *The Count of Monte Cristo* was released in 1934 with a plot that hinges on redeemed outlaw Edmond Dantès escaping from his island prison and carrying out his revenge.[35]

This one's tricky, because the story has multiple lawmen who all view their assigned outlaws as irredeemable and disposable. One of those lawmen is Dantès's warden, who whips everyone in the prison once each year for amusement. Another, the prosecutor who had Dantès arrested on trumped-up charges, is so incapable of seeing the good in those he considers outlaws that when Dantès confronts him years after the frameup, he doesn't even recognize him outside the context of prison. *The Count of Monte Cristo* also contains multiple redeemed outlaws, including the main character, Dantès, as well as his incarcerated friend, Abbé Faria, who earns his redemption by helping Dantès escape, and by dying in the process (plus he hooks Dantès up with the location of a treasure, making him rich). The outlaw and the lawman are not always restricted to a single character. The archetypes bleed across various identities in some stories, but always in the character of the outlaw is a thirst for redemption, and always in the lawman is a desire to withhold it.

The 1939 film *Convict's Code* told the story of outlaw Dave Tyler (Robert Kent), who encounters numerous lawmen, including the warden and his parole officer, after he is sent to prison for a bank robbery which he claims he did not commit. These lawmen lean into their stereotypical distrust and constantly remind Tyler of his guilt despite his persistence of innocence. When they meet for the first time, the warden responds to Tyler's claims by saying, "in all my experience, I've never bumped into the case of convicting an innocent. I'm still waiting for the first one."[36] After his release, his parole officer encourages him to stop pursuing an acquittal and accept his guilt in an effort to move on with his life. It isn't until the film's conclusion, when he is granted a pardon from the governor, that viewers discover, along with the warden and the parole officer, that Tyler was indeed innocent.

In 1940, *Castle on the Hudson* pitted mobster Tommy Gordan

against Warden Walter Long inside New York's infamous Sing Sing Prison.[37] Before Gordan is convicted of robbery, he believes he is above the law, and he is confident his attorney will manage to secure his release without much trouble. When that doesn't happen, Gordan finds himself stuck in a world where he is expected to follow the rules just like everyone else. He eventually earns his redemption by taking the blame for a murder committed by his girlfriend, winding up on death row despite his innocence. The film concludes with his death at the hands of the state, a performance I will unpack in upcoming chapters.

The 1957 film *Jail House Rock* follows redeemed outlaw Vince Everett (Elvis Presley) to prison after he accidentally kills a man in a bar fight.[38] Everett learns how to play the guitar while in jail, and when released on parole, he attempts to follow through with his dreams of becoming a performer. But he confronts a host of obstacles related to his incarceration. The lawmen include not only the guards who Everett constantly fights while in prison, but also the toxic traits he picks up while incarcerated, which become a hinderance as he attempts to build his singing career after release. Films that follow the outlaw beyond prison only to find them still struggling with the emotional baggage of incarceration present a metaphoric version of the archetypal lawman that is inescapable regardless of release, redemption, or even exoneration.

The Bird Man of Alcatraz is a film based loosely on the life of redeemed outlaw Robert Stroud, and when it was released in 1962, one film critic praised it as "one of the finest pieces of film-making to come out of Hollywood in many a disappointing day . . . an astonishing tour de force."[39] After the film's obstinate lawman, Warden Shoemaker, refuses his mother a visit, Stroud retaliates by killing a guard. The violent act fuels the lawman's refusal to offer redemption when it appears to be earned later in the story through acts of kindness and self-improvement. A big part of Stroud's redemption is accomplished by showing us his love of birds, and as viewers, we begin to feel like maybe he isn't as awful as we first thought.

In 1967, *Cool Hand Luke* introduced movie-goers to decorated veteran Luke Jackson, who is sentenced to prison for drunkenly stealing parking meters.[40] The producers made it easy to like Luke; his offense is petty, and his status as an ex-sergeant in the Army gains him the support of US audiences early into the film. Given his victimless crime, we don't really find ourselves wishing him punished at all, so he begins the story halfway to redemption in the eyes of viewers. And like most of Paul Newman's characters, we only grow to like Luke more as the story progresses. The archetypal lawman in *Cool Hand Luke* is a sharp-shooting guard with a quick trigger-finger who eventually murders Luke during a failed escape attempt. The lawman who refuses the outlaw his redemption has many avenues at their disposal, but one of the most common is the killing of the incarcerated.

Viewers were also treated to Robert Aldrich's *The Dirty Dozen* in 1967, a story about a group of twelve men, each sentenced either to life in prison, or to death.[41] The film follows their attempts to regain their freedom by accepting a dangerous mission that will almost certainly end in their deaths. Colonel Everett Breed is the story's lawman, a strict leader who won't entertain the possibility that a group of incarcerated men could prove successful at anything other than crime and mayhem. In a conclusion that seems to both confirm and reject the colonel's beliefs, offering death *and* redemption (or perhaps redemption *through* death), the surviving outlaws trap a group of German officers and their mistresses inside of a bunker, douse them in gasoline, then ignite them with a grenade. The assault is a success, but only a single outlaw survives the mission to regain his freedom and, presumably, his redemption.

In 1974, *The Longest Yard* won a Golden Globe Award for best picture in the category of musical or comedy.[42] It was so popular it was rebooted in 2005 starring comedian Adam Sandler. The film tells the story of redeemed outlaw Paul Crewe, a former professional quarterback who is sentenced to 18 months in prison for stealing his girlfriend's expensive car, then drunkenly (and intentionally) driving it into a lake.[43] In prison, Crewe agrees to coach a group of other incarcerated players in a football game against the guards, who already have a well-trained team. The film's obstinate lawman is Warden Hazen, who threatens Crewe with additional trumped-up charges unless he intentionally loses the climactic competition, a move rooted in the lawman's refusal to accept the possibility of an outlaw with redemptive ethics. Crewe's girlfriend is portrayed as a cliché spoiled brat, so we almost appreciate Crewe for drowning her expensive car; but he truly gains our support as the final football game plays out. In a comical scene where Crewe proves his loyalty to his team, he is flagged for two subsequent penalties after he intentionally throws the football at a guard's crotch, and then has the entire team pile on top of him. The guards almost win the game, until a last second, one-yard run—the longest yard—puts the outlaws ahead as time runs out.

In 1979, *Escape From Alcatraz* presented the semi-biographical story of outlaw Frank Morris (Clint Eastwood), who is convicted of bank robbery and sent to Alcatraz Federal Penitentiary.[44] Roger Ebert described the film as "a taut and toughly wrought portrait of life in prison," one that reveals "the ways of dehumanizing that are peculiar to this prison."[45] Our redeemed outlaw has a rough go of things from his first night in Alcatraz, when he is marched through the cellblock naked, then locked in his cell as a guard quips, "Welcome to Alcatraz." As the film unfolds, Morris is pitted against both his fellow prisoners, who wish to harm him, and the prison staff, who refuse to intervene and protect him. When he is targeted in a sexual assault and a subsequent attempted murder, his only solution appears to be an escape. The obstinate lawman in *Escape from Alcatraz* is the nameless warden, who is unable to accept the apparent success of the prison break, insisting instead that Morris and his co-conspirators drowned.

In 1981, John Carpenter's *Escape from New York* dragged the genre of prison film into the realm of science fiction with outlaw Snake Plissken, played by Kurt Russel. The story kicks off with Air Force Once crashing in a dystopian Manhattan, which has been walled off from the rest of the world and classified as a maximum-security prison. Snake's mission requires him to rescue the President from the other residents of the island prison, returning him to the land of the free and, in the process, earning his own freedom (and redemption). The film's lawman is Police Commissioner Bob Hauk, who repeatedly threatens Snake's life if he attempts to leave Manhattan without first rescuing the President. He doesn't expect Snake to be successful, but he does expect him to dodge his agreement and attempt to escape New York when no one is watching. The archetypal lawman lacks the capacity to expect anything except additional criminality in the outlaw.

Perhaps the most infamous prison film of all time, *The Shawshank Redemption*, premiered in 1994, pitting outlaw Andy Dufresne against the prison's obstinate lawmen, the warden and his gang of dirty guards. Andy attempts to gain his redemption by proving his innocence, but the warden is unwilling to entertain it, even when a witness shows up who can exonerate him. Unwilling to let this outlaw be freed, the warden has the witness killed. Andy's redemption only comes by escaping through a sewer pipe, literally crawling through human waste. Co-star and fellow redeemed outlaw "Red," played by Morgan Freeman, only escapes by telling the parole board (his obstinate lawmen) that he is no longer seeking redemption. *Then* they let him go, as if the purpose of prison lies in forcing the outlaw to join the lawman's side and accept their irredeemable nature.[46]

Dead Man Walking premiered in 1995, introducing consumers to a third archetype in prison film—the sympathetic, often religious volunteer who acts to buffer the tension between lawman and outlaw. Sometimes it's a mother or sibling. Sometimes it's a lawyer. In this film, it's Sister Helen Prejean, played by Susan Sarandon. Prejean serves as a religious guide to those awaiting execution on death row, including the film's archetypal outlaw, Matthew Poncelet, played by Sean Penn. In *Dead Man Walking*, the twist comes when we discover the main character is indeed guilty despite his longstanding persistence of innocence, and a form of redemption is achieved when he confesses to Prejean just before his death. Storylines that paint the prison system as ultimately effective and necessary despite its harshness reveal a consequence of prison media which I will unpack in upcoming chapters.

In 1996, *Sling Blade* became what Nellis calls "arguably the first of a series of movies which quite explicitly placed personal redemption at the heart of the released prisoner narrative," presenting a picture of a convicted felon who wants to "go straight," and "also feel[s] compelled to make amends for harm done, to atone."[47] The main character, Karl Childers, is released from a criminal asylum after serving 20 years for murdering his mother and her lover in a confused rage. His redemption is completed in true Hollywood fashion when he discovers that a neighborhood child and his mother are being abused by a man who lives with them, so he murders the abusive boyfriend and winds up back in the custody of the film's symbolic lawman, the criminal asylum.[48]

Childers provides an interesting example of the irredeemable nature of the outlaw being used as a sort of redemptive strategy. By turning his violence against those who viewers feel deserve it, like detective-murderer *Dexter* or contract killer *Barry*, this outlaw manages to achieve something like redemption without ever showing remorse or changing his ways.[49] He simply directs his irredeemable outlaw nature toward a worthy target; he victimizes people who viewers *want* to see victimized.

Also in 1996, Michael Bay directed *The Rock*, a film which followed redeemed outlaw Captain John Mason (Sean Connery) through an adventure set largely in Alcatraz "The Rock" Penitentiary.[50] The story's obstinate lawman is FBI Agent Stanley Goodspeed (Nicholas Cage), who keeps Mason on a short leash after signing him out of a different prison to help him save San Francisco (and possibly the world) from a band of rogue marines-turned-terrorists threatening to release toxic gas if their demands are not met. Mason gains his redemption not only by fixing the problem and saving lots of lives, but also by risking his one shot at escape by attempting to rebuild a connection with his daughter, who he hasn't seen in years. The trope of the outlaw who is humanized by his connection to family is far from original, and it works to build our support for the redemption the outlaw eventually earns by the end of the film.

In 1998, *American History X* was praised by *The New York Times* as a film that presents a "bold but reckless synthesis of visual enticement and rhetorical fever" in a way that "dares to address America's neo-Nazi culture with brutal candor."[51] The film's archetypal outlaw is Derek Vinyard (Edward Norton), the leader of a Neo-Nazi gang in Los Angeles. During the three years he spends in prison for a racist murder, Vinyard experiences a polar change in his belief system, although not until after he is gang raped by white supremacists in retaliation for befriending a black man in prison.[52] Helen Eigenberg and Agnes Baro note that *American History X* "uses rape as a central theme to motivate major change in the main character," thereby causing viewers to have compassion for Vinyard because of the horror he experiences in prison.[53] The obstinate lawman in *American History X* is the prison itself, especially the extreme violence and racism Vinyard encounters while locked up, which appears to be endorsed by the system as a whole. I will unpack the consequences of such representations in upcoming chapters, but it's important to note that Vinyard's redemption comes largely from the cruelty he endures while in prison, not from rehabilitative programing or deliberate self-improvement. He is effectively abused into redemption.

In 1999, Eddie Murphey and Martin Lawrence starred in the prison comedy *Life*.[54] They both play redeemed outlaws who find themselves trapped by a system that not only appears unwilling to release them despite their clear innocence, but also seems set on abusing them until the day they die. The obstinate lawman in *Life* is the entire correctional system, although some cogs in the machine play a much more pertinent role than others. In this case, the legal system is an easy target, considering the film is set in 1932 and the outlaws are both black men. The Jim Crow connections allow viewers to understand that these two outlaws do not deserve to be in prison in the first place, so their redemption is easily earned long before they escape at the end of the movie.

In 2000, *Oh Brother, Where Art Thou?* rebooted Homer's epic Greek poem the Odyssey into a 1937 Mississippi setting.[55] There are three outlaws in this film, and they work as a team. The story begins with them running away from prison, having escaped from a chain gang assigned to break rocks on the road. The film's lawman is Sheriff Cooley, who attempts to hang the outlaws even after the governor issues them a pardon. Even though the majority of *Oh Brother, Where Are Thou?* is set outside prison, it still relies on the same tropes of outlaw and lawman to drive the plot. It's not unusual for outlaws to find their way to the free world at some point in the story, and like Valjean, to use their freedom as an opportunity to earn redemption.

In 2001, *The Last Castle* told the story of General Eugene Irwin, played by Robert Redford, who is court-martialed and sent to a maximum-security military prison.[56] Once there, he butts heads with the film's lawman, Colonel Winter, played by James Gandolfini. Winters rules his prison with an iron fist, abusing and even killing those inside, and nothing infuriates him faster than a threat to his unquestionable power. True to character, when Irwin begins to organize a group of incarcerated men, earning their respect and upsetting the normal power dynamic, the lawman resorts to murder, first Irwin's followers, and eventually Erwin himself. The hero who lays down their life for the cause is another trope that is older than Hollywood.[57]

In 2002, Omar Epps starred in *Conviction*, a film based on the life of outlaw Carl Upchurch.[58] The script follows Upchurch through childhood and into prison, then into habitual recidivism. This outlaw seeks redemption through education, eventually earning degrees both inside and outside of prison. The obstinate lawman is Sheriff Stark, who at one point shows up to a home where Upchurch is staying after release from prison and tells the homeowner, "This man is beyond rehabilitation; he needs to be watched very, very carefully." Despite continued arrest, including one just for driving to South Philadelphia, in the end, Upchurch wins his redemption by organizing a nationwide gang summit in Kansas City to broker a peace agreement.

Jim Sheridan's 2005 *Get Rich or Die Tryin'* is loosely based on the story of rapper Curtis "50 Cent" Jackson, who plays the role of Marcus, the story's redeemed outlaw.[59] Marcus is a drug dealer who winds up in prison, where he learns that his girlfriend is pregnant with his child. He subsequently challenges the obstinate lawman, portrayed as the social system that provided him few options other than drug sales, then sentenced him to prison for his misbehavior. Marcus manages to polish his talent for rapping, and once released from prison, he pursues what Nellis describes as "redemption through art" by managing to disengage himself from the drug trade and maintain a legal lifestyle.[60]

In 2005, Fox's television series *Prison Break* hit prime time with redeemed outlaw Michael Scofield.[61] The show begins with Scofield botching a bank robbery to get himself sent to prison, where his real goal is to break his brother out. In a twist, his brother is also a redeemed outlaw of sorts, a shady character who was framed for the murder of a high-profile politician, but who is nonetheless guilty of several other crimes. The obstinate lawman is played by a mysterious organization with limitless resources and faceless leaders known only as "The Company." We don't know who they are, but we do know they are unwilling to allow the outlaws in this story any chance of achieving their redemption, regardless of what it takes to keep them locked up.

These archetypes are not genre specific, but they are perhaps most evident in comedic representations of the prison environment, like the 2006 film *Let's go to Prison!* starring comedians Dax Sheppard and Will Arnett.[62] Arnett plays the redeemed outlaw who is sent to prison for stealing an inhaler while having an asthma attack. While incarcerated, he is sexually assaulted and tortured in various scenes (all in a comedic framework to minimize audience cringe). Meanwhile the film's obstinate lawmen, played by Dax and the always-bored employees of the system, drive the plot by setting the archetypal outlaw up for constant trouble.

In 2009, Jim Carey played redeemed outlaw Steven Russell, who falls in love with fellow outlaw Phillip Morris (Ewan McGregor) after being sent to prison for stealing. The film is *I Love you Phillip Morris,* and it follows Morris and Russell as they both seek redemption, albeit through different routes.[63] Morris becomes the traditional penitent prisoner who is eventually released and begins building a new life, fulfilling what I will refer to as prison as penance in upcoming chapters. Russell, on the other hand, spends the entire film repeatedly breaking out of prison, often using clever methods and complicated ruses to secure official releases—a trope which I will later refer to as prison as a playground. The prison setting and the long arm of the law play the obstinate lawman in the film, and at the end, when Russell is thrown into solitary confinement ("The Hole") for the rest of his natural life, the obstinate lawman appears to win, permanently excluding Russell from any possibility of redemption. But Russell achieves something like redemption anyway, for the film wouldn't feel concluded if he didn't. The script is based on a true story, and as the final scene ends, viewers learn (in text) that the prisoner who inspired it has decided to stop escaping after five unsuccessful attempts; he is yielding to the system, giving up his rule-breaker identity and acquiescing. You might call it redemption.

In 2010, one of the prisons where I (the author) spent time became the set of a film called *Stone,* starring Robert DeNiro, Milla Jovovich and Edward Norton.[64] The Michigan State Prison in Jackson, Michigan was the largest walled prison on Earth when it began housing state prisoners in the 1930s.[65] The walls are so massive that those who stay there are housed *inside them,* in cell-blocks where producers of *Stone* manufactured their big screen magic. In the film, Norton's character, Stone, works with a parole officer named Jack Mabry (DeNiro), who also acts as the film's lawman. Stone's major goal is to get out of prison, and Mabry's main goal becomes keeping him locked up, although his motives start to seem a bit suspect part way through the film, when Mabry starts sleeping with Stone's girlfriend in the outside world. Stone is finally granted his parole, but in the end, viewers are left wondering if his redemption is short lived, since the lawman's house mysteriously catches fire the night our outlaw is released.

Throughout the first century of prison cinema in the United States, women have seldom been featured in big-budget productions set inside prisons. The problem is gender, or rather, how audiences expect to see gender performed on screen. The fights, riots, rapes and abuses which drive the plots of prison films about men don't work as well in representations of a women's prison; patriarchal norms of protection (and domination) won't allow a mass audience to enjoy that sort of suffering inflicted on women's bodies. Jenji Kohan broke that cultural taboo in 2013, when she found a way to play on those same gender norms in *Orange is the New Black (OITNB)*.[66] Since she couldn't pedal in the hyperviolent spectacles often used to spice up men's prison films, Kohan instead manufactured a divide between the prison setting and a new arrival who has no idea what she is getting into. This prison space *feels* confusing and threatening based on the main character's apparent innocence and vulnerability.[67]

The redeemed outlaw in *OITNB* is Piper, a middle-class white women locked up for a nonviolent crime she committed long ago. She is completely unfamiliar with the rules and etiquette inside prison, and viewers can't help but laugh as we follow her through bumbling mistakes in things like the chow hall, prison bartering, race relations, and just interacting with others inside. It's hilarious, and that's why the series works. The majority of those watching

Netflix and other streaming services in the United States are (still) white, middleclass consumers who don't have much personal experience with prison.[68] Such viewers take comfort in the outlaw's discomfort, because she mirrors our imaginary reactions; she does what most of us would do in the same situation. Piper's innocence works to make the tame-for-Hollywood prison setting feel more threatening than it actually is while also preserving the sense of safety obtained from being on this side of the screen.

The obstinate lawmen in *OITNB* include various wardens and administrators who are so abusive that a prison riot erupts in season 3. And here, again, Kohan works the magic of intersecting gender, race, class and able-bodiedness on screen in such a way that nonviolent situations and toned-down fights feel intense and dramatic despite lacking the mayhem and gore of male prison violence. We still *feel* like we are watching a prison film because the main character is so out of place in what appears to be a prison environment. Kohan explained the trick of using Piper as both bait and buffer on an episode of NPR's *Fresh Air*:

> "In a lot of ways Piper was my Trojan Horse. You're not going to go into a network and sell a show on really fascinating tales of black women, and Latina women, and old women and criminals. But if you take this white girl, this sort of fish out of water, and you follow her in, you can then expand your world and tell all of those other stories."[69]

This wasn't the first time Kohan managed to build a Hollywood women's prison environment. The comedy series *Weeds,* which began an 8-season run in 2005, includes brief depictions of the main character, a woman, in prison serving a 3-year sentence.[70] And it's not hard to spot where Kohan's original ideas for *OITNB* were born. The few short prison scenes which introduce the seventh season employ many of Kohan's best tricks, including an outlaw who is a woman encountering confusing situations that make her (and us) feel uncomfortable, and a climactic scene where the entire cellblock cheers as the outlaw passionately kisses another woman.

In 2013, Arnold Schwarzenegger and Sylvester Stallone teamed up as two redeemed outlaws in *Escape Plan*, pitted against the film's obstinate lawman, Warden Hobbs, an underhanded character who is ultimately killed in the final escape attempt.[71] The two main characters find redemption through entwined narratives. Breslin (Stallone) was only in the prison because he was hired to test its security, and his redemption is gained when he reestablishes his freedom and his prior identity. Rottmayer (Schwarzenegger) gains his redemption by reestablishing a relationship with his daughter, who ultimately aids in the final escape. The film was a success, considering in 2018 its sequel starred many of the same characters.[72]

In 2017, the latest film remake of the 1962 book *Papillon* was released. It follows redeemed outlaw Henri "Papillon" Charrière through the horrors of several violent experiences in prison as his repeated escape attempts fail.[73] He eventually survives a jump from high cliffs into the waves below, escaping and, in the process, regaining his redemption, which comes to a conclusion with the publication of his book. The story reads (and views) like a moral indictment of the prisons and lawmen discussed, along with the governments which utilize them. Charrière's redemption comes from publishing the story, which he narrates.

In 2022, Bruce Willis starred in *Corrective Measures* as Julius "The Lobe" Loeb, an outlaw in a supernatural maximum-security prison packed with werewolves, cyborgs and monsters.[74] Loeb is hiding a huge fortune in untraceable assets, and the film's lawman, Warden Devlin, played by Michael Rooker, is dedicated to forcing the outlaw into telling him how to access it. Loeb achieves something like redemption at the film's conclusion, when he uses his superpower to take over the crooked warden's body and escape, leaving the lawman locked up in his place.

This brief journey through nearly a century of prison film verifies the archetypal characters of the redeemed outlaw and the obstinate lawman, who have been repackaged and then resold over and over as different characters in "new" movies. Despite their apparent idiosyncrasies, each portrayal continues to display similar characteristics. They have become Jungian archetypal representations—characters who can vary a great deal in detail without losing their basic pattern.[75] We know them so well that introductions aren't necessary, a boon to writers who are saved the hassle of drawing those lines in for us. In addition to the tried-and-true archetypes of the redeemed outlaw and the obstinate lawman, contemporary television shows and films that focus on imprisonment have fostered the evolution of a cliché prison setting, as producers have discovered that the formula for cinematic gold relies on certain key ingredients. The success of these films depends on the ability of their creators to emphasize aspects of the prison environment that viewers find entertaining, while neglecting features that viewers find unpleasant, distasteful or boring. In a culture obsessed with spectacles of destruction and stories of infamy, that's a real problem.

Chapter 2

Prison as a Character

"Brutal state practices are therefore legitimated through narratives that frame the punitive treatment of prisoners as both necessary and deserved."[76] —Bill Yousman

"Societies have always been shaped more by the nature of the media by which men communicate than by the content of the communication."[77] —Marshall McLuhan

An overhead shot reveals a massive facility of brick and mortar, surrounded by towering walls topped in razor wire, and packed with shuffling bodies who all seem to be going nowhere. A buzzer sounds and a gate opens, sliding roughly across a track that hasn't seen oil in years. Those already inside the fences line up to jeer and shout at the newcomers, creating a twisted welcome wagon for both new arrivals and those of us watching from home. It's metallic and loud from the second we arrive, and once we head inside the building, it also gets dark and cavernous. Everyone appears to be glaring at everyone else, and those in charge are cruel, or even violent when they don't immediately get their way. There are threats around every corner—violence, sexual assault, exploitation—and the entire prison appears divided into racial cliques who all seem ready for war. Unlike the world outside of prison, those who are best at abusing others are esteemed by nearly everyone else; evil men become role models here. It's creepy and dark, but for some reason we really want to watch more. Welcome to the world of prison on screen. The spectacle of punishment will commence shortly.

According to the United States Department of Justice's Bureau of Justice Statistics, around 4% of state and federal prisoners report experiencing at least one incident of sexual victimization by either staff or others who are incarcerated each year.[78] While unacceptably high, this number represents a small minority of incarcerated people. But you wouldn't know it from watching prison films, where sexual assault is a go-to for scriptwriters looking to draw in an audience. Sex sells, even if its violent and uninvited.

It should come as no surprise that, as hooks explains, "Homophobic construction of gay sexual practice in mass media consistently reinforce the stereotypical notion that gay folks are predators, eager to feast upon the innocent."[79] But when cinema depicts the space of prison, viewers often expect to encounter a special kind of evil. It's so common to see sexual assault in depictions of correctional environments that we are seldom surprised when such storylines play out. Eigenberg and Baro found that "while most studies on male rape in prison suggest that it is a relatively rare event," in contemporary movies, "the inclusion of at least a reference to male rape and/or a peripheral rape scene has become a standard part of prison film production."[80]

It's not just the men who are exploited as sexualized characters. Dawn Cecil recognizes a similar (albeit misogynistic) formula at work in scenes with women in prison: "These 'babes-behind-bars' films perpetuate highly sexualized images of female prisoners . . . It is Hollywood, after all; they do not necessarily seek to educate—instead they aim to titillate."[81] Leonidas Cheliotis went even further in *Crime, Media, Culture,* where he described the fictional prison setting as a place where:

"Imagination tends to be taken on a sensational journey into spaces where the false and the fictional arise victorious from the ashes of the real. Prisons are usually typecast either as dark institutions of perpetual horror and virulent vandalism or idyllic holiday camps offering in-cell television and gourmet cuisine on the back of taxpayers."[82] Television and film representations of the prison environment reinforce problematic stereotypes regarding incarceration while minimizing aspects of imprisonment that fail to sufficiently entertain an audience.

It's more than sexual assault. Prison cinema plays on all our worst fears and deepest frustrations with human nature. Prisons on screen aren't just cages. Once the lights are set up and the cameras are rolling, prisons are magical spaces of terror and spectacle where viewers can travel at will without fear of physical harm or emotional trauma.[83] The following chapters will track the emergence and growth of three archetypal prison settings used to house the outlaw and the lawman of contemporary cinema: prison as a playground, prison as penance, and prison as a paradox. These tropes frequently work together, bolstering one another in what feels like the natural progression of a story. Most commonly, cinematic outlaws new to the prison environment must learn confusing rules and withstand hazing (paradox). At some point they frequently experience some sort of brutal assault (a playground for the assaulter). In the aftermath of the violence, producers shift seamlessly into the practicing of lesson learned (penance), a progression which often incudes a change of heart wherein the outlaw attempts to be a better person, or at least a better prisoner. It is the same story each time, packaged differently and performed by new actors, yet echoing the same tired tropes as always.

Cheliotis's institutional "idyllic holiday camp," which I shall refer to as prison as a playground, is exemplified in scenes depicting prison murder, rape, or drug sales as daily occurrences in prisons and jails.[84] These crimes represent many of the behaviors prisons are supposed to dissuade, so scenes depicting them taking place inside a prison suggest that, for at least some of the convicted, rules can always be circumvented. The playground trope is also reinforced any time viewers are shown images of luxury or excess in prison, like the scene in Scorsese's film *Goodfellas* where "wise guys" eat lobster in prison, or the prison in *Suicide Squad* where Harley Quinn's cell has a cappuccino machine and a sound system playing classical music.[85] It's also wound up in representations of the guy who can get you anything, as Red describes himself early into *The Shawshank Redemption*. Unfortunately, as viewers, we can't help but walk away from such depictions feeling like the prison system just isn't strict enough; if it could just clamp down a bit harder, perhaps the monsters contained within it might be prevented from wreaking the havoc we see on screen.

Despite the violence and mayhem frequently depicted in cinematic prisons, in the end, the punishment machine is shown to be ultimately successful in its attempts to rehabilitate (or at least contain) most dangerous characters, a trope which I shall refer to as prison as penance. The trope of prison as penance portrays the penitentiary as a terrible-yet-necessary place where bad people serve their well-earned punishment, often on their way to redemption. If all goes well, outlaws are eventually returned to public life, while those who remain imprisoned indefinitely are products of their own behavior—bad guys of the worst sort designed to strike terror into the hearts of viewers. The end result in depictions of prison as penance is redemption of the mainstream variety, usually portrayed as sorrow, regret, changes in one's ways, and volunteering to help others avoid a similar path. Despite terrible experiences and confusing mistakes, the redeemed outlaw in a prison as penance story learns something from their incarceration, leading to a better life after release. Often the penance one experiences goes far beyond what we would normally consider disciplinary, from torture to sexual assault sustained at the hands of other incarcerated people. When the end result of such stories is a change of heart, viewers come to accept prison as a valuable tool of discipline, believing that although it might be rough (at times even torturous), it is at least effective in forcing a reevaluation of one's ethics. And in those rare cases when even the worst punishment available fails to change the outlaw's ways, prison as penance is always willing to cage the worst bad guys until the day they die, protecting viewers from the characters on screen who might otherwise haunt us in our sleep.

A third recurring representation of prison on television and film focuses on the confusion and systemic ineffectiveness of the prison institution. Representations of prison as a twisted game where villains enforce confusing rules provide examples of what I shall refer to as the trope of prison as a paradox. When we chuckle at a "don't drop the soap" joke, prison as a paradox is bearing fruit. When we see something that just doesn't make sense—drinking wine brewed in a toilet, pocket-holding on the yard, unpunished sexual assaults, tattooing with dangerous equipment, murders over petty mistakes, breakout attempts with just a few days left on one's sentence—we come to understand prison as some sort of confusing game of victimization, and we view those in prison as evil, manipulative players beyond redemption. It does not make sense to be sexually assaulted for dropping the soap, and we all know it; we wouldn't put up with such weak script writing in any other setting. Yet as viewers of a prison film, we uncritically accept puzzling accounts of victimization. It is, after all, prison. Unconsciously, such scenes work to reinforce our beliefs about how awful those inside prisons must be if they can survive such a confusing, brutal experience: *I'm sure glad that guy doesn't live next door to me.*

There is a silver lining to the trope of prison as a paradox. Unlike representations of prison as a playground or prison as penance, prison as a paradox opens a space for viewers to consider the prison industrial complex as an ineffective machine of torture that is so confusing and misguided it seldom produces little aside from trauma and grief. These three archetypal prison settings (playground, paradox and penance) are the main ingredients in prison movies and television shows regardless of genre or era. They make the cinematic prison and those within it entertaining.

As Hollywood has consistently sought to outdo itself with each new film or television production, the tropes of prison as a playground, prison as penance, and prison as a paradox have been refined and adjusted to satisfy evolving consumer demands. Not only must a brutal prison rape in a new movie outdo the brutal prison rape from the last movie, but it must also appear to be part of an original plot. This prison riot must appear different than the last; this breakout attempt must somehow premier as a new spectacle. As we consume these stories over and over, each feeling slightly different than the last, we slowly build a collection of knowledge related to prison—what Michel de Certeau called a "referential reality" that, at times, takes the place of real information which we cannot acquire from our position outside prison.[86] We might be capable of balancing that information out with real accounts of imprisonment, if we had them. But who wants to go to prison and spend a few years learning how it really works?

In truth, it wouldn't matter if you did go to prison to balance out your Hollywood library, because cinematic representations have also been shown to affect the perspective of individuals *who themselves have been to prison.*[87] Humans use films and television shows to make sense of our lives, and to explain our stories to others. In a Hollywood-happy culture like the United States, that's a real problem. The typical prisons of contemporary cinema not only reinforce the perception that the prison industrial complex is indispensable, but they also suggest the necessity of its continued expansion and permanent harshening if society is to remain free from the threat of dangerous and malicious criminals. For those of us who have been to prison, those same narratives become handy tools for explaining our past experiences to others, or for finding common ground when discussing a subject. An average US citizen might not have any personal experience with an actual prison, but they probably have hours of experiences with the same films we have seen. It makes sense to begin with our common ground and to work outward from there. As hooks explains, "movies not only provide a narrative for specific discourses of race, sex, and class, they provide a shared experience, a common starting point from which diverse audiences can dialogue about these charged issues."[88] Our media diet is infecting our cultural understanding of prison and those who live there, teaching us to fear those behind bars and leading to our calloused treatment of folks who we come to see as monstrous others, different from us in virtually every way.

The Spectacle of Punishment

The Biblical book of Matthew tells the gruesome story of John the Baptist's death.[89] During a drunken party, King Herod was so enchanted by the erotic dancing of a young woman that he offered her any gift she requested. After discussing her options with her mother, she decided she wanted the head of John the Baptist delivered to the party on a silver platter. At the time, John the Baptist was still alive, locked in a Roman prison for crimes against the state. The gruesome execution of the prophet and the subsequent displaying of his severed head provided entertainment for a room full of the King's party guests. Two thousand years later, the story survives, providing an early example of the spectacle of punishment, in this case, execution as a source of entertainment, with a plot driven by an intoxicated King's libido.

Not only had the spectacle of punishment been around for thousands of years by that point, but it continued to evolve throughout the next two millennia. Jewish law at the time stipulated the spectacle of public execution for a number of other non-violent "crimes," including blasphemy, adultery, and even homosexuality.[90] Executions typically occurred in public venues, and they were frequently carried out at the hands of the citizenry via the spectacle of stoning: the public would throw rocks at the accused until they were dead.[91] These social events served multiple purposes; they were entertainment for voyeurs, a warning to anyone who might consider similar violations, and of course, a hands on experience for those who wished to participate in the killing by throwing stones at the condemned. Although the modern-day Bible does not explicitly describe these events as exciting or entertaining, the fact that numerous societies recognized similar laws and carried them out for thousands of years is evidence of the long-standing social acceptance of the spectacle of punishment.[92]

The surviving Biblical accounts are far from unique. Discipline and punishment have always been used by those in positions of power to ensure that those who might otherwise threaten their authority are kept in check.[93] For much of our history, the more graphic the display of violence, the better. After all, public executions are about keeping the community in line as much as they are about disciplining individuals. But as states progressed into more contemporary nations and jurisdictions, many such acts of public violence were eventually declared illegal. Nonetheless, state-sanctioned violence as punishment for a crime remained a spectacle that served to satisfy what Sigmund Freud referred to as "The natural instinct of aggressiveness in man," which "opposes this program of civilization" when left unregulated.[94] With the invention of contemporary law, humans would no longer be responsible for parsing out our own justice. We must now seek relief through the "program of civilization," also known as the legal system.

For much of human history, our mechanisms of discipline targeted the body of the accused through execution or torture. But the last few centuries have seen a slow, steady shift toward targeting the mind (and the reputation) of the accused through public shaming and dethroning. As Michelle Alexander makes clear, *The New Jim Crow* is about permanent stigma, not paying one's debt to society: "the system primarily depends on the prison label, not prison time."[95] The two progressions have gone hand in hand; as we've advanced from personal vendettas and self-governance to states that monopolize discipline and violence, we've also advanced from brutal, public events meant to torture the body of the accused to hidden institutions of mental and emotional torture cloaked in brick walls and razor wire. Public violence has evolved into secluded torment, while physical discipline has evolved into spiritual condemnation.

In the opening paragraphs of *Discipline and Punish: The Birth of the Prison,* Michel Foucault describes a grisly scene from the mid-eighteenth century where a man convicted of murder was publicly executed after being tortured before the townsfolks: he was beaten, burned with sulfur, ripped to pieces with red-hot pinchers, quartered by horses, and eventually burned to ashes.[96] Antebellum America adopted a similar attitude toward the public spectacle of punishment. William Penn believed that corporal punishments were more than just appropriate, but were also, as Hartnett explains, "useful public performances, literally theatrical plays demonstrating that elites would use violence to create political order."[97] After the Civil War, the stubborn institution of white supremacy normalized extralegal spectacles of punishment, including the lynching of black people accused of petty crimes, often without any evidence. These violent events were as popularized as the executions of old, and as Harold and DeLuca explain, "In these lynching pictures, crowds of whites pose with the mutilated bodies ... dressed in their Sunday best ... Lynching was an event, an occasion to see, to be seen, and to memorialize for others."[98]

The spectacle of photography allowed participants to partake of the event on more than one occasion—to take it with them and have a bit later on, or to share it with a friend. More importantly from our perspective, it allowed those of us who see these photos today and in the future to study them, and to make accusations concerning those pictured. These spectacles of punishment have become indictments of our cultural history, as well as indictments of many of our ancestors. Images testify to the horrors of extralegal executions, the glee of whites participating in illegal torture, the lack of remorse or forethought given to posing in photographs that would long outlast the posers, and the taken-for-granted dehumanization that informed such behavior. In short, cultural artifacts which survive allow those who study them to unpack the cultural history of whatever is performed or preserved within them.

The public stood witness to such spectacles of violence and punishment, including public torture, hangings, and beheadings, until well into the 19th century, when, according to Foucault, the emphasis on judging the body began to be replaced with an emphasis on judging "the soul of the criminal."[99] The increased ease with which images could be reproduced and distributed led to, among other things, the condemnation of those who participated in illegal lynchings and mob violence. We moved from punishment societies to discipline societies, and in so doing, we began to discipline *ourselves* in most cases, constantly performing assigned cultural roles to avoid additional mechanisms of restraint common to our era. The social media shaming and doxing of today might look very different from the gallows and stocks of the seventeenth century, but they are both a form of public discipline. Humans have used this method of control ever since social rules were created and were, shortly thereafter, broken.

The self-discipline most of us work so hard to perform is of no interest to a subset of any group. Their rule breaking is the reason spectacles of discipline persists, often in the form of violence, whether executions, arrests, forced movement, or slave labor.[100] A distinction persists, however, between portrayals of violence that are state sanctioned and legal, and those that are not. As Max Weber infamously proclaimed, "one can define the modern state sociologically only in terms of the specific means peculiar to it, as to every political association, namely, the use of physical force."[101] Citizens are largely restricted to non-physical discipline, whereas the state has a monopoly on violence.

Of course, that violence takes more than one form, but it has long since moved from the pillory, where we might have paused to throw a tomato or laugh at the accused, to the screen, where we enjoy our dinner while watching incarcerated people experience torture at the hands of the prison and one another.[102] The result, as Brown explains, is that "a shadow world of moral judgement and penal logics exists beyond prison walls as a constant and perpetually growing cultural resource for people to make sense of punishment."[103] We use those television shows and movies to make sense of our world. Unfortunately, when the spectacle of punishment is engaged, our empathy and humanity are muted, or even deactivated outright. They only get in the way of the fantasy. The comfort of the screen allows us to shut them down and enjoy the show.

Our social consumption of punishment porn is reinforcing our calloused acceptance of the US prison industrial complex, which currently houses a full 20% of Earth's prisoners and soaks up nearly 10% of annual US budgets.[104] It has become normal in the United States to devote massive sums of energy and cash to locking rule-breakers in dungeons, then leaving them there indefinitely, considering two-out-of-three released prisoners are rearrested within 10 years.[105] Prisons, it turns out, are better at (re)producing criminals than at rehabilitating them. A big reason for the US's seemingly permanent recidivism problem has to do with how we feel about those in prison. As Ray Surette suggests, "...people use knowledge they obtain from the media to construct a picture of the world, an image of reality on which they base their actions," a habit that "is particularly important in the realm of crime, justice and the media."[106] We love spectacles of violence and punishment, but we hate to be reminded that our vice has consequences. Our lust for the salacious is fueling our problem with mass incarceration.

The world we live in and the world we enter on television are not only related; they are reliant upon one another. As McRobbie and Thornton have shown:

> "Social meanings and social difference are inextricably tied up with representation. Thus when sociologists call for an account which tells how life actually is, and which deals with the real issues instead of the spectacular and exaggerated ones, the point is that these accounts of reality are already representations and sets of meanings about what they perceive the 'real' issue to be."[107]

If humans didn't enjoy spectacles of bloodshed, crime and

punishment so much, *Oz, Prison Break* and *Orange is the New Black* would have flopped. Our media diets betray us. But all is not lost, for we can keep our precious Hollywood machine and our overpriced popcorn at the big screen while redesigning it to rid ourselves of the pesky hatred we seem to have developed for people in prison.

Chapter 3

From the Street to the Screen

"natural ignorance has been replaced by the organized spectacle of error."[108] —*Guy Debord*

"the technique of reproduction detaches the reproduced object from the domain of tradition. By making many reproductions it substitutes a plurality of copies for a unique existence."[109] —*Walter Benjamin*

"Desire has the power...to make us forget who we are. It both disrupts and deconstructs. It dismembers and disembodies."[110] —*bell hooks*

The spectacle of punishment has long since moved from the street gallows into the walled penitentiary, where it now remains stubbornly hidden from public view. Instead of official beheadings and crucifixions held in town squares, the spectacle of punishment is now presented via television and movies, commodified for Adorno and Horkheimer's "aesthetic mass consumption."[111] The penitentiary walls that keep prisoners in also keep the eyes of the public out, but the film reproduction of a prison environment casually discards this bothersome censor. When we think about prison nowadays, we think about the movies we have seen, the books we have read, and the television shows whose release dates we anticipate. It is easier, safer, and more comfortable to view prison through a screen than to visit an actual prison, and the sheer number of prison films produced during the last century confirms viewers still enjoy such vicarious trips to the penitentiary. As Brown has suggested, "It is in these spaces that much of the popular knowledge about punishment is constructed—in spaces far from the social realities and the social facts that define mass incarceration."[112]

Representations of prisons on screen cause those who watch them to feel as if we are experiencing an actual prison environment, but they also preserve the sense of safety and security that comes from being cozy in our living rooms. As Cheliotis suggests, "The inherent artificiality of media exposure to crime helps neutralize the incipient sense of personal danger, without preventing evocation of it as real and grave."[113] Unfortunately, the safety-buffer of media comes at a high cost: consumers lose touch with the real world. When viewers are exposed to events and environments that would normally produce a sense of trepidation, the safety of the screen allows for the temporary disabling of such emotions because the danger is not real. It is only an illusion. The more we see it, the more normal it becomes, until eventually it is what we expect to see.

Prison and the spectacle of punishment are now key components of the culture industry, providing many consumers with the only source of information available regarding the penitentiary.[114] We learn about prison from film and television, relying on producers and set builders to construct representations that align with reality. And in the end, we take what they give us, consuming the spectacle as is. Media spectacles are currently monologues, permanent one-size-fits-all productions unable to be updated or challenged by consumers once they are finalized in the studio. That may change in the future, but for now we can only learn what we are given.

Media images are political images; per hooks, "No aesthetic

work transcends politics or ideology."[115] There is always a story being told in any picture regardless of how unbiased or objective a photographer is attempting to be. It's bigger than just television and film. As Harold and DeLuca show in their description of Emmett Till's murder and subsequent media proliferation:

> "In 1955, the photographic image of Emmett Till's corpse put a shocking and monstrous face on the most brutal extremes of American racial injustice . . .the grisly image of his corpse . . . became a crucial visual vocabulary that articulated the ineffable qualities of American racism in ways words simply could not do."[116]

Whenever we see something that moves us to action, or that causes us to feel as if something should be done, we have been politically motivated, whether the producers of the image meant it or not.

As Michel De Certeau argues, "Today, fiction claims to make the real present, to speak in the name of facts and thus to cause the semblance it produces to be taken as referential reality."[117] Television has an uncanny ability to produce imaginary spaces that feel as if they are real—productions masquerading as reality. Shawshank Prison does not exist. It is a figment of Stephen King's imagination projected through producer Frank Darabont onto a dilapidated state prison facility in Mansfield, Ohio.[118] But *The Shawshank Redemption* is a movie (and a short story) that takes viewers into the bowels of a high-security, twentieth century prison. For those who have never been inside of an actual prison, the dark scenery and violent atmosphere serve to provide a point of reference in the absence of any real personal knowledge—Certeau's "referential reality."[119] These islands of remembrance pop up when we need them in the future, whenever someone mentions solitary confinement, fresh fish, or "don't drop the soap." Movies not only entertain us, but they also rewire us. "Representations colonize the mind and the imagination," according to hooks.[120]

The prisons on our screens increasingly become the prisons in our imaginations, and we use them to make sense of the world. They are, after all, the only prison many of us know. Sure, we realize it's fiction. We understand it's a story created solely for enjoyment, not education. Yet that knowledge evaporates once the opening credits roll, and the prison, along with the actors who occupy it, evolve into a space which the viewer experiences as reality, inseparable from any other memory one might have of some experience from the past. In the future, when we are put in a situation where personal knowledge of prison is required, we "refer" to whatever scraps of information we possess, spitting out fragments of Hollywood narrative and confusing them as real knowledge. Adorno and Horkheimer's prediction from 1947 came true; "Real life is becoming indistinguishable from the movies . . . the film forces its victims to equate it directly with reality."[121] Our lives have become a jumble of real and fake, true and illusion.

The Dance of Art and Life

Sometime during the fourth century B.C., Plato described how "Art imitates life" in Book X of *The Republic:* "The imitator or maker of the image [artist] knows nothing of true existence; he knows appearances only."[122] According to Plato, artists are not required to learn nearly enough about the objects and ideas which they plan to include in their paintings, sculptures or other art to truly do those things justice in their re-presentations. In constructing art, says Plato, the artist must learn *only* enough to present an acceptable facsimile, a copy fit to satisfy those with minimal knowledge of the subject matter. If you want to convince someone that the Eifel Tower is far from the city, or that Stonehenge is in the middle of town, just show them pictures of these landmarks artistically drawn (or "Photoshopped") into the wrong locations. So long as they don't know any better, your representation will become their standing truth. If you want to make viewers believe that prison is full of monsters who sexually assault one another and constantly attack guards, create media with these places artistically produced to overemphasize the macabre. In the absence of any personal information to balance out the artistic misrepresentation, the caricature becomes truth in the minds of consumers. The artist, according to Plato, is responsible for this miseducation and should, therefore, think twice before producing anything that might mislead their audience. Since we can never know what portion of our art someone might misunderstand, or what proportions we might inadvertently get wrong, we should hesitate to create *anything* artistic for fear of lying to our fans. This from a man who spent much of his life creating stories by weaving dialogues into philosophical prose: an artist.

Two millennia later, Oscar Wilde flipped Plato's assertion around to claim that "Life imitates Art far more than Art imitates life," suggesting that mankind's insatiable "desire for expression" feeds upon itself: "Art is always presenting various forms through which this expression can be attained. Life seizes on them and uses them, even if they be to her own fault."[123] Although the two statements seem at first antithetical, Plato and Wilde both agree that the artistic representation is only a simplified version of some original, and more importantly, that the representation provides the otherwise uninformed viewer with a set of alleged facts which might easily be recalled at a later time as truths rather than as artistic representations. Fredric Jameson took this concept a step further, ominously suggesting that the commodification of culture would leave future societies reliant on these narratives as a source of historical knowledge: "we are condemned to seek History by way of our own pop images and simulacra of that history."[124] Life imitates art, then art imitates life; they dance with one another in a never-ending waltz of genealogical leftovers, a trail of crumbs we can follow to make sense of the world we currently occupy. The age of social media has made crystal clear the axiom that life imitates art, *and* that art imitates life; it's a cycle. We see someone's social media post about an adventure—their art imitating life—so we want to go on an adventure—life imitating art—and then we take our own photo to post on social media, creating art that imitates life that was already imitating art, *ad infinitum.*

Of course, with social media, the stakes are often low. You might try to copy your friend's adventure only to realize that Plato was right and their photo made something appear much easier or smaller than it turned out to be. But you have the experience anyway, and in the end, you learn that your original beliefs were not quite correct, so you adjust them to align with new information. With prison films, we usually lack the ability to balance out fiction with experience, so instead, we just take for granted the truth of violent plotlines and bizarre behavior. We might think they are overrepresented or exaggerated, but we still accept that they are based in truth. Our world becomes the world we see on screen, because, per hooks, "even though most folks will say that they go to the movies to be entertained," most of us go to the movies "to learn stuff. Often what we learn is life-transforming in some way."[125] The transformation is not always a positive one. D.W. Griffith's promotional film for the KKK, *The Birth of a Nation,* likely transformed some who saw it, but not in any fashion that advanced equity or feminist politics of the day.[126] Media spectacles can mislead just as well as they can educate. When scripted scenes take place in a prison, our critical reasoning is deactivated, and horrific events don't necessarily affect us the way they should. We are, after all, witnessing the ghastly space of prison; we know what to expect from our prior consumption of mass media.

Take, for example, scenes of sexual assault in male prison movies, which should cause viewers to oppose harsh punishment if things were as simple as art imitating life. Since most viewers already know, wrongly, that prisons are packed with sexual assaulters, such scenes not only make sense without us giving them much thought, but they also work to *reinforce* the legitimacy of the prison system by reminding us (wrongly) just how terrifying those inside prison are. Dialectical tensions drive plotlines because humans love to see people get what they've got coming to them, so when the prison system appears designed to ensure the abuse of Hollywood-style monsters who are incarcerated within its walls, we don't mind so much.

Prison cinema plants and waters the seeds of uncritical support for the prison industrial complex. As Cheliotis explains, "Rather than undermining the external legitimacy of prisons. . . media representations reinforce public perceptions of the overall essentialness of the prison institution and of the essentialness of its further growth and harshening."[127] Travis Dixon has shown that, when it comes to cinematic prison portrayals, "stereotypes tend to be both self-fulfilling and self-perpetuating precisely because they help us explain the world."[128] And Sue Mahan and Richard Lawrence said it succinctly in *The Prison Journal:* "When it comes to crime, media coverage *is* socially constructed reality."[129] Since actual penitentiaries are essentially censored from public oversight, "media coverage" provides the most prominent source of information concerning the silent and hidden world of prison operations. Our junk-food diet of media is teaching us everything we believe we need to know, leaving us woefully misinformed.

Updates in the Spectacle

The evolution of the cinematic prison has resulted in three motifs that consistently emerge in prison representations, occasionally in isolation, but usually in combination: prison as a playground, prison as penance and prison as a paradox. Each television show and movie examined in this book will present a picture of an archetypal prison setting, as each was chosen to serve as what Communication scholar Kenneth Burke called a "representative anecdote," a story that is "supple and complex enough to be representative of the subject matter it is designed to calculate," yet simple enough to provide an overarching framework that fits other similar stories.[130] Representative anecdotes are valuable tools for understanding the objects they portray, and in the case of cinematic representations of prison, any event that is left out of the program says just as much about the film as the events that are included. Viewers demand these reductions, for most movies and television shows would be far too lengthy and banal if every second of the main character's life was included. It is the events emphasized and those ignored which create the very fabric that holds the movie plot together, and prison film producers consistently choose the most scandalous and horrific accounts of bad behavior writers can conjure up.

Burke expounded on his idea of selective focus, explaining that humans:

> "seek for vocabularies that will be faithful *reflections* of reality. To this end, they must develop vocabularies that are *selections* of reality. And any selection of reality must, in certain circumstances, function as a *deflection* of reality."[131]

That's a mouthful, but all Burke really means is that language has power, and the way we *talk* (or don't) about something has a lot to do with how we ultimately *feel* about it. Take the German word *schadenfreude*, which, loosely translated, means the process of experiencing joy from someone else's suffering. English doesn't have a comparable word, an absence which many wrongly consider evidence that English speakers do not take as much joy in the suffering of others as German speakers do. But Burke's "deflection of reality" explains the intentional lack of that term in English representations of the world, for the existence of the word makes it possible to talk about the thing. Finding enjoyment in the suffering of others, especially our enemies, is about as human as it gets. Our lack of language in this specific area is likely strategic silence, not oversight. Speakers of English are not morally superior to speakers of German; we are just more willing to deceive ourselves and ignore our unsavory characteristics. We use more nuance and, as such, more language to describe the same process, usually while protecting ourselves from the icky feelings of guilt which might come with admitting our enjoyment in another's misfortune. Humans are storytellers (even to ourselves) above all else.

De Certeau's referential reality comes down to the information we have and the information we lack in the moment, in that split second when we are asked to think about a prison and an image comes to mind. Brown has discussed the "penal subjectivity" we experience as a result of our media diet: "performances of punishment, when distinct from actual punishment, nevertheless provide frameworks for ordinary citizens to step into or out of self-conscious modes of awareness as moral spectators and deliberative citizens."[132] Television and movie tropes of prison as a playground, prison as penance, and prison as a paradox are each a Burkean "reflection," "selection," or "deflection" of reality. Producers of prison cinema choose to portray certain aspects of incarceration, while underemphasizing others and ignoring some completely. The viewer's "penal subjectivity" is, in the end, dependent on choices made by writers and Hollywood executives.

More than a half-century has passed since Burke first coined his idea of selective focus, and the largest advancement in television and film production involves the improvement of technology, namely, digital editing software and special effects. While producers can manipulate scenes and add realistic digital content easier than ever before, viewers have more entertainment options and can access information faster than ever before. Images that appear on screen are increasingly unreliable, even as they continue to become easier to access and more realistic.

Steven Shaviro describes this phenomenon in his book, *Post Cinematic Affect,* where he summarizes the history of media technology, from the films of the early twentieth century to "newer media—television, video, and a whole panoply of computer-based forms" which are now our main source of information about the world.[133] New modes of production, digitization, and improved special effects have created a new standard of production that is further than ever from reality. As Shaviro explains, these new forms of media:

> "provide indices of complex social issues . . . but they are also productive in the sense that they do not *represent* social processes, so much as they participate actively in these processes, and help to constitute them. Films and music videos, like other media works, are *machines for generating affect* . . . they generate subjectivity, and they play a crucial role in the valorization of capital."[134]

Rather than acting as a simple representation of an object, Shaviro believes films actually help to create and reinforce a set of feelings and opinions related to the objects portrayed—that there is a direct relationship between things we see in films and our subjective beliefs and feelings about those things. We don't just think a certain way about prison and those who live there; we *feel* a certain way about that place and those people. And our feelings are powerful. They motivate us to update our opinions, or to double-down on what we have believed all along. Movies create culture then hide their tracks by reflecting it back at us.

As with any commodity, images that elicit a desirable affect in the viewer become our favorites, and conversely, images that do not elicit the desired emotional response will be subsequently passed over for alternatives that may produce the desired affect (and effect). Producers of any commodity, including prison cinema, must meet standards that satisfy consumer demands, or else the consumer will simply choose a more satisfying substitute. There are more options on offer every day. The spectacle of punishment has joined the ranks of commodity, streaming ceaselessly into the homes of consumers via television sets, computers, smart phones, and tablets.

As Guy Debord notes in *Society of the Spectacle*, "The spectacle is the moment when the commodity has attained the *total occupation* of social life."[135] Once the representation of the prison environment, as depicted via Shaviro's "new media" representation, becomes a source of knowledge to the viewer, there is no need for additional information: "The real consumer becomes a consumer of illusions. The commodity is this factually real illusion, and the spectacle is its general manifestation."[136] As the proliferation of mass media continues unchecked, the spectacle of punishment will continue to evolve along with it, carving out an expansive space of supplemented reality which the viewer is enticed to accept as fact in the absence of any additional information. We are learning to fear our neighbors and to take pride in our burdensome prison system.

This slippage between an actual prison and its cinematic representation leads to real world consequences. As we have already seen, when free citizens come to believe that those in prison are violent, incorrigible monsters barely contained by the prison system, we naturally want to keep them there, and to harshen the punishment they are receiving. As this examination of the tropes of prison as a playground, prison as penance, and prison as a paradox unfolds, keep in mind this dialectical tension between the real and the spectacle, which is teaching us to fear those in prison and to endorse their poor treatment. The fact that even those of us who have spent time in prison resort to media representations to make sense of our stories and to share them with others suggests not only that these narratives fill in missing pieces of information in our comprehension of the world, but that, in some cases, they have the ability to *replace* real accounts of prison.[137] When the source for society's information concerning criminal corrections consists solely of cinematic spectacles, the necessity of sustaining and expanding the current system is unquestionably reinforced. As Yousman explains, "These brutalizing fictions suggest that the penal system is too lenient or soft ... [that] even more policing and surveillance is necessary ... even harsher prison environments and sentencing policies."[138] Recurring tropes of the prison environment in media tacitly reinforce a cultural belief in the necessity, continued growth and harshening of the prison industrial complex.

Chapter 4

Prison as a Playground

"In popular entertainment, journalistic exposés, and documentaries, images of 'life behind bars' fascinate, horrify, and titillate. They also offer a familiarity with prison as a cornerstone institution of modern life, but one that the majority of people never enter. The nonincarcerated public comes to recognize prison and the imprisoned almost exclusively through a set of rehearsed images created by the state and by nonincarcerated image makers—images like arrest photos, mug shots, the minimal furnishings of the prison cell, fortress-like walls, barbed wire, bars, metal doors, and the executioner's chair."[139] —Nicole Fleetwood

"giving audiences what is real is precisely what movies do not do."[140] —bell hooks

"the instant the criterion of authenticity ceases to be applicable to artistic production, the total function of art is reversed. Instead of being based on ritual, it begins to be based on another practice— politics."[141] —Walter Benjamin

Our journey into the trope of prison as a playground for demented monsters begins with FOX's hit television series *Prison Break*.[142] The show premiered new episodes for a total of five seasons between 2005 – 2017, winning numerous awards during its prime time run, including a People's Choice Award in 2006.[143] False convictions and clandestine escape plans dominate the main plot, while a constant barrage of violence and mayhem keeps viewers occupied as the story unfolds. A big part of the show's success stems from horrific depictions of human depravity, which *USA Today* found noteworthy in their reviews, especially "the racism, violence, and sexually predatory behavior" of the redeemed outlaw's "dysfunctional fellow prisoners."[144]

Prison Break, as the title suggests, is the story of a group of men who conspire to break out of prison. The redeemed outlaw is Michael Scofield, a wealthy businessman who inexplicably robs a bank during the first episode. He surrenders when police show up, and after a brief trial where he refuses to defend himself against the wishes of his attorney, he winds up in Fox River State Penitentiary.[145] It is here that the real plot begins to take shape. Michael's brother is incarcerated in the same facility, falsely convicted of murder and awaiting execution. The show evolves as Michael's plan to break both he and his brother out of the prison slowly comes together. In the meantime, viewers get to meet all sorts of stereotypical prison characters, including a redeemed outlaw, an obstinate lawman, and a host of unrepentant monsters whose acts of mayhem and violence drive the plot.

Like the original archetypal outlaw, Valjean, Michael and his brother appear doomed to remain ensnared in a correctional system that refuses to release its firm hold on them despite their well-earned redemption. Viewers learn shortly into the series that Michael only committed his crime to help his brother escape before his execution, which is only a few weeks away. Producers chose well when casting actor Wentworth Miller (Michael), whose soft-spoken nature contrasts with the harsh, Hollywood prison environment while still maintaining a sense of control in the violent space. He is easy to cheer for; he committed a crime in which no one was injured, his motives appear noble and desperate, and we uncritically sympathize with him from the story's outset. He's a good guy who is just trying to save his brother from a conspiracy aimed at taking his life. The employees and the warden of the prison, on the other hand, exude the archetypal lawman's typical obstinance, refusing to consider the possibility of the outlaw's innocence. They are all surrounded by a host of villains versed at manipulating the system inside the maximum-security prison to turn the correctional space into their playground.

Monsters in the Background

Theodore Bagwell, known by those in prison as "T-Bag," is a recalcitrant prisoner who acts as one of the prominent antagonists in *Prison Break*. He is a proud white supremacist, a flagrant sexual predator, and a convicted rapist-murderer who is esteemed by a large following of other white supremacists inside the prison.[146] Shortly into the series he is introduced to another character by someone who admires him: "you best speak with respect, fish. The man kidnapped half a dozen boys and girls in Alabama, raped and killed them—wasn't always in that order either."[147] It is revealing that T-Bag's character works so well, for most people understand, rightly, that folks convicted of sexual assault have a particularly difficult time in prison, and even following release.[148] The idea of a sexual predator gaining notoriety by taking pride in his crimes should strike us as ridiculous, but we have learned well what to expect with our prison films. T-Bag is just par for the course in representations of prison as a playground. As Steinmetz and Kurtz have discussed in their work concerning mainstream media of all sorts, characters who indulge in hedonism and violent, masculine destruction:

> "live out a kind of male fantasy in which they
> pursue absolute decadence while lamenting how
> relationships and social conventions rein in their
> desires. Movies like *The Hangover* series, *Animal*

House, and *Old School* capture a kind of masculinity that uses up the body, disregards the consequences, and lives for the moment outside the demands of women and basic civility."[149]

In prison films, this trick is simply taken to the extreme. Producers of *Prison Break* flaunt what other shows must play with in jest, because in prison we expect the characters to behave poorly.

Bagwell is the latest in a long list of cinematic stereotypes who thrive in the prison environment and revel in their roles as unapologetic shot-callers unable to be fully contained by incarceration. In the course of the first season alone, T-Bag perpetrates a number of sexual assaults on other characters, incites a prison-wide race riot, and eventually murders one of the guards to avoid disciplinary sanctions.[150] He is Hollywood red meat, the sort of monster that leaves viewers on the edge of our seats. We want to see him get what's coming to him. We also want to see what he will do next. But more than anything else, we just want to zone out and be distracted from our lives, which is always the real point of fictional cinema. As hooks reminds us, no matter how hard we attempt to watch something with a critical eye, there is typically at least a short time when we are "seduced . . . by the images we see on screen. They have power over us and we have no power over them...if we were always and only 'resisting spectators,' . . . films would lose their magic."[151] We click on the screen and click off our critical reasoning because that's how movies and television work. You don't add them to your own story and create your own ending; you hop on and enjoy the ride, or you complain about the mistakes you spot along the way (as media critics often do, to the chagrin of our fellow viewers). Once we play along and follow that script, the programs we consume, in many ways, consume us, bleeding into our memories and incorporating themselves into the fabric of our being in the process.

T-Bag is more than just a character inside the prison. His nickname is a euphemism for a sexual act which is forbidden in the prison environment, and in many ways, he actually represents the trope of prison as a playground in the flesh.[152] His debauchery is a reflection of the world producers wished to convey to the audience, a reminder that prison is a place full of rulebreakers and sexual predators. His very name brings to mind the playground atmosphere producers were looking to create.

In *The Shawshank Redemption,* a similar stereotype is represented in a group of predators led by a man named Boggs. These thugs wander around the prison at will, and from time to time they sexually assault other incarcerated characters without many consequences, a storyline that intersects with that of the film's redeemed outlaws.[153] Producers left little doubt as to how we should feel about these rapists, who are recurring characters in prison cinema. We are encouraged to see them as inhuman, and when Boggs is eventually beaten so badly that he is permanently injured, we hardly pity him; he is, after all, a monster who could not be stopped any other way. In one scene, when the movie's narrator, Red, hears a potential victim ask, "I don't suppose it would help any if I explained to them that I'm not homosexual," he casually responds, "Neither are they. You have to be human first; they don't qualify." Even the other incarcerated characters understand they are surrounded by evil monsters who are incapable of redemption; they don't even view them as human.

The Sisters and their leader, Boggs, are a gang that thrives in the contained environment of Shawshank Prison. By committing gang rapes and sexual assaults throughout the film while immune from the pesky oversight of officials, they manipulate the rules of the system in the contained spaces within the prison walls to create and utilize a power dynamic that leaves their victims at a disadvantage. They make the prison into their playground, and they seem right at home in even the most restrictive environments. As viewers, what are we to think except that even the most secure facility on Earth is still too nice for these guys, who we want to keep locked down forever. If only prisons were a bit stricter, perhaps T-Bag and The Sisters might be prevented from hurting others.

Two years after the release of *The Shawshank Redemption,* the cable television network HBO raised the bar on hyperviolent prison spectacles when it began airing episodes of the television show *Oz*.[154] Most of the scenes take place inside a maximum-security prison housing unit, and the characters are a collection of murderers, rapists, aggressive criminals and colluding guards. The program frequently depicts scenes of violence, conspiracy, and prison rape, leaving viewers with the impression that these activities are prison norms rather than isolated incidents. *Oz* is the expresso of prison spectacle, a reduction of the typical trope of prison as a playground. Producers removed the banal and mundane, leaving nothing but the violence, depravity, and macabre, and presto, they had a hit.

Author Elayne Rapping contends that the hyper-violent depiction of the prison setting in *Oz* "presents a vision of hell on Earth in which inmates are so depraved and vicious that no sane person could possibly think they should ever again be let loose upon society."[155] *Oz, Prison Break,* and *The Shawshank Redemption* introduce audiences to worlds that are alien to most and dangerous to all, and in so doing, they give viewers the impression that an hour of prime time television represents a typical day in prison. Instead of walking away feeling as if we have consumed a fictional account of mayhem, we wind up feeling like we have experienced something realistic and authentic.[156] That's the "magic" of Hollywood.

Even the bizarre feels real when we see it on screen. But as Yousman explains, "*Oz's* purported 'realism' is therefore not only fictional, but fictional in ways that reproduce the worst stereotypes about prisons and prisoners."[157]

Prison cinema provides viewers a glimpse of a horrifyingly violent world, one far too terrifying to allow anywhere near you and your loved ones.[158] *Oz* epitomizes the trope of prison as a playground, framing the correctional environment as an elaborate and ever-exciting spectacle fraught with drugs, violence, and depraved entertainment—aspects that, while occasionally present in prison, are far from premier characteristics. The trope of prison as a playground, as demonstrated through *Prison Break's* Bagwell, is expanded to comprise the entire group known as The Sisters in *The Shawshank Redemption,* and enlarged yet again to incorporate nearly the entire prison population (and some of the guards) in *Oz.* Whether the playground is represented through the behavior of a single bad apple or the entire prison population makes no difference, for the impact is the same: we come to think of prison as a demented and menacing world easily manipulated by those inside who wish to continue victimizing others.

Bagwell provides the starkest example of prison as a playground in *Prison Break,* but many of his fellow actors also aid in the creation of the environment. And since producers had already cracked the door on peddling in stereotypes, they followed through with additional characters who made social justice advocates cringe. John Abruzzi, the leader of an Italian American mob family, is serving a life sentence for several crimes, including murder. Abruzzi's reputation and his wealth land him the coziest job in the prison, and he continues to run his criminal operation during his time behind bars. He orders the murders of numerous enemies, he has two of Scofield's toes cut off, and he eventually chops Bagwell's hand off with an axe during an escape attempt gone awry.[159]

Abruzzi adds to the sense that prison is a twisted playground for those who have the right connections. The rules that govern the behavior of most do not seem to apply to him because of his mob ties. Of course, those who have seen films like *Goodfellas* or television shows like *The Sopranos* know this archetype all too well—the untouchable mob boss who keeps a stash of lobster and cigars throughout his prison sentence.[160] At times, Abruzzi seems free to perpetrate nearly any act he wishes in the prison, as long as he does not leave the facility. He frequently conspires with Brad Bellick, an officer at Fox River who viewers see collecting money from incarcerated characters in exchange for various illegal services. A "dirty" guard presents a particularly poignant addition to the trope of prison as a playground, as even those in a position of authority become part of the twisted game.

The story's redeemed outlaw, Scofield, is perhaps the shrewdest example of a character who understands the prison to be a playground and uses the rules to his advantage, up to and including escape. Throughout the series, Scofield is presented as intelligent, observant, and always one-step ahead of everyone else. His redemptive qualities include his genius, his ability to get people out of difficult situations, and most importantly, his willingness to give his life for his brother. Early into the series, it is revealed that Scofield has a massive tattoo that covers his entire torso, from his neck to his waist. The images are convoluted and abstract, including large, distorted angels and demons locked in fierce battle, surrounded by archways and crisscrossing patterns. Later in the series, viewers learn that the tattoo is in fact an elaborately concealed copy of the prison's blueprints, interwoven with intricate artwork to prevent its detection.[161] Prior to his arrest, Scofield intentionally branded the prison's blueprints onto his body so they could not be taken from him, and he concealed them so they would not be detected.

Scofield's body holds more than just hidden blueprints. During one episode, he decrypts a tattooed recipe for a strong corrosive that can be made with products available in the prison, and then he uses the chemical to burn a hole through a pipe.[162] In another, Scofield uses a razor blade to slice into his forearm and remove a hidden pill, which he later delivers to his brother in a plot to forestall his execution.[163] Scofield's tattoo also holds a number of additional "keys" to the eventual prison break, including the make and model of a screwdriver needed to remove a prison toilet, the name of the streets that will be traveled during the escape, a contact's coded phone number, the passcode for a combination lock, and even the GPS coordinates for a safe house outside the prison. His body becomes a metaphoric map out of the playground, and he uses his tattoo to flow through the restricted space of incarceration effortlessly.

Rather than painting the redeemed outlaw as a victim of the playground, such as in films like *The Shawshank Redemption* and *American History X*, in *Prison Break* the redeemed outlaw is shown to use the trope of prison as a playground to his advantage. Scofield's ability to smuggle the information he needed into the prison, and to utilize it appropriately throughout the series, was all part of an ultimate plot, the fruit of well-laid plans. The story only makes sense if one thinks of prison as a playground that is so predictably gameable one could hack it from the outside. Prison as a playground is the sort of place taxpayers want to crack down on, reducing funding or forcing stricter methods of discipline. We certainly don't want things to get any easier around that place.

In *Fast & Furious 8*, ex-cop Luke Hobbs, played by Dwayne "The Rock" Johnson, gives us an image of prison as a playground when he is locked in the same maximum-security facility as his archrival, bad guy Deckard Shaw (Jason Statham).[164] The action in this playground for hyperviolent men reaches a crescendo when Hobbs and Shaw are unexpectedly released from their cells and wind up in a fight with each other, along with dozens of taser-wielding guards dressed in full body armor. Since the trope of prison as a playground relies on evil monsters who are always a threat to social order and nearly impossible to subdue, producers opened all the cell doors along with those of the two main characters, setting the monsters free. Unsurprisingly, all-out war ensues when everyone comes charging out to immediately attack the guards and one another, because that's what incarcerated people are like in the movies. A stereotypical Hollywood prisoner is not only hyperviolent, but also hard to contain and incredibly strong, a trope performed by Hobbs when a few guards shoot him with a beanbag shotgun. First, the bullets bounce off his chest without injury. Then he quips, "rubber bullets; big mistake" before throwing one guard across the room and shooting another with his own gun.

Depictions of prison as a playground often include a predictable collapse into the chaos of a riot. In *Prison Break,* we learn by the end of the pilot episode that Fox River is on the verge of a race riot, yet another stereotype that plays well with the trope of prison as a playground. Riots require combatants. What's more, they require planned targets. And they require a lot of both. It isn't a riot if everyone isn't beating up everyone else. When we view these depictions over and over, we can't help but think there is some morsel of truth to them. Scenes depicting mass prison violence as a regular occurrence remind us, wrongly, that prison is full of victimizers who are always plotting an attack and waiting for the right moment to pounce.

Prison as a playground is by far the most common trope in

prison cinema because producers rely on keeping an audience's attention, and playground material is fun to watch. The options are nearly limitless. It's simple things, like obtaining privileges or restricted items, but it's also more intense scenes, like the drugs that seem to be easily available in prison or the ease with which people can sexually assault one another and get away with it. And it's most visible when it's made to be visible, like happens in comedy.

Chapter 5

Fresh Fish, Sadistic Guards and the Cushion of Comedy

"When we laugh over a delicately obscene witticism, we laugh at the identical thing which causes laughter in the ill-bred man when he hears a coarse, obscene joke . . . hilarious humor . . . weakens the inhibiting forces among which is reason, and thus again makes accessible pleasure-sources which are burdened by suppression."[165]
—*Sigmund Freud*

"Contemporary film editing is oriented, not toward the production of meanings (or ideologies), but directly towards a moment-by-moment manipulation of the spectator's affective state."[166]
—*Steven Shaviro*

"Laughter opens the door to perception. It allows a thought to get in because you are completely unguarded and Zen-like when you are laughing."[167] —*George Carlin*

As the preceding section has shown, the trope of prison as a playground, reflected through irredeemable characters who thrive in institutional spaces, has been distilled to the level of pulp characterization. The continued success of the films already discussed reveals the ongoing ability of hyperviolent spectacles of punishment to entertain contemporary audiences, but as their "R" and "Mature Audience" ratings suggests, the characters that result from this process are often too evil for a general audience to enjoy.[168]

But something strange happens when macabre subject matter is wrapped in a cushion of comedy, and suddenly the fear associated with a horrible event, such as the shanking or raping of a character, becomes palatable. Sigmund Freud spoke of this power, which is inherent to comedy and wit, claiming that "the main character of wit-making is to set free pleasure by removing inhibitions," a process which "affords us the means of surmounting restrictions and of opening up otherwise inaccessible pleasure sources."[169]

Researchers have now advanced Freud's theories on wit, finding that when participants tell a positive joke just before explaining an upsetting picture, like an image of a car accident or an injured person, they experience fewer and less intense negative emotions then when the joke does not precede the explanation.[170] Humor, it seems, forces a change of perspective by initiating psychological adjustments which cause us to reevaluate things we normally classify as negative without much thought. The cushion of comedy allows contemporary audiences to accept what would otherwise strike them as taboo or disgusting; it disables any visceral emotions that might restrict us from enjoying a distasteful scene.

Kenneth Burke's work on framing reminds us that the way a story is told has a lot to do with how people feel about the mistakes a character makes along the way. According to Burke, crime stories are typically framed in one of two ways: dramatically or comedically.[171] When we view a story through a dramatistic frame, we see the outlaw as violating the hierarchy of authority, acting in "conflict with established values," and therefore threatening social order, which we (as rule-followers) have a stake in protecting.[172] Dramatistic frames make us long to see the bad guys in crime stories punished and restrained to prevent social chaos, and to protect ourselves. But when we instead view a story through a comedic frame, Burke believes we replace the dramatic monsters in our imagination with tragic clowns, and he invites us to view "people not as vicious, but as misguided."[173] When we think of those who commit crimes as comedic fools who made bumbling mistakes, it becomes much easier to forgive them than it is to forgive their dramatic counterparts. We replace our anger with compassion, and our desire for revenge becomes an empathetic connection with people who are just like us. This, in Burke's view, opens a space for rethinking taken-for-granted policies of punishment based on revenge, the norm in the United States.

As A. Cheree Carlson summarizes, "The clown is created not to serve as an enemy, as in tragedy, but as an example."[174] Carlson goes on to unpack the value of Burke's theory: "The clown embodies all the problems of the social order, but even as s/he is separated from the herd, we recognize a 'sense of fundamental kinship,' a knowledge that everyone 'contains [the clown] within.'"[175] The empathy we experience when someone tells us a clown story is powerful. We hate the dramatic troublemaker and wish to see them punished; we love the tragic clown and wish to see them earn their redemption: "When the clown is punished, dialogue can begin, eventually leading to rapprochement. Clown and society remerge in a newly repaired social order."[176] The way a story is told has much to do with how we feel about those within it. Comedy has the unique ability to declaw difficult topics, allowing conversation to move into spaces that are otherwise off limits. It deactivates our anger and judgement, replacing it with curiosity and compassion. And in that state of mind, we can rethink taken for granted norms, we can challenge accepted stereotypes, and we can engage in thinking experiments that are otherwise impossible.

In Hollywood, producers take advantage of the cushion of comedy to create enjoyable stories and characters that would otherwise infuriate public audiences. And from time to time, buried within those scripts are messages and challenges which we prefer to avoid thinking about. The cushion of comedy works both ways; it can dull our empathy as easily as it can enhance it, depending on how it is implemented and where it is directed. Unfortunately, comedic cinema set inside a prison often offers an easy out when it comes to true consideration of the topics depicted. Unsanitary conditions, solitary confinement, violent treatment and even sexual assault can lose their shock value when presented in a comedic frame, becoming just normal, everyday occurrences in the prisons of our imagination.

Comedic Outlaws

Cheech and Chong began their thirty-year run of comedy films in 1978 with the cult classic *Up in Smoke.*[177] Cheech and Chong films are all built around the cushion of comedy, constructed by leaning into stereotypes of drug use that allow us to laugh at the bumbling fools on screen, even when they do things we would otherwise find reprehensible. The redeemed outlaws (Cheech and Chong) are classic stoners. Too high to notice their nonstop mistakes, they leave a path of destruction wherever they go, crashing cars, lighting buildings on fire, and causing damage to personal property. Yet beneath our chuckling at their antics, they are incredibly dangerous citizens whose bad behavior doesn't trigger typical judgmental responses in viewers because producers have cushioned their crimes in comedy. The jail scenes in *Up in Smoke* included representations of prison as a playground, including drug dealing guards, drunk judges, and oblivious street cops who are uninterested in doing their job. We are laughing as we watch, so we don't engage our critical thought, and the scenes pass without any real consideration of the consequences of a police department and a jail staffed with such characters. The comedy wouldn't work if we were busy criticizing people who don't exist, so we jump on board the storyline and enjoy the show.

The 2009 film *I Love you Phillip Morris* dragged the trope of prison as a playground into classic Jim Carey styled comedy, allowing for some over-the-top depictions of depravity that avoided the criticism they otherwise might have received. The entire film is based on the ineptness of the prison system and the ability of one outlaw to disable its hold on him with minimal resources and a little luck. The prison is shown as a classic playground in various ways, including one scene where a man publicly masturbates during a movie night, another where steak and lobster are procured by the main character, and numerous scenes where incarcerated characters are shown cuddling and having sex, which are both against the rules in prison.[178] There is even one scene where a man who struggles with mental illness and "screeches" every night, to the chagrin of those in the cellblock, is savagely beaten by another prisoner who was paid to commit the assault. In response to the violence, the main character's boyfriend says, "that's the most romantic thing anyone ever did for me." The only reason we can abide the brutal assault on someone we should feel sorry for is because it is immediately followed by a joke, easing the tension. Nonetheless, both the assault and the joke undergird our preexisting understanding that prison is a place full of violent monsters who don't feel empathy for their fellow humans. And of course, the requisite casual sexual assault is depicted when at one point a character says to another, "so do I need to suck your dick?" and is met with the response, "yeah, that'd be great." It's all just business as usual when the cushion of comedy runs through the trope of prison as a playground.

Bruce Helford's comedic television series *Anger Management* aired weekly on FX from 2012 – 2014.[179] According to a review in *Rolling Stone* magazine, the show's first episode "drew a record-breaking 5.47 million total viewers," which at that time made it "the most-watched debut in FX history."[180] The show follows counselor Charlie Goodson (Charlie Sheen) as he leads an anger management group inside a prison. Prison as a playground is the show's main theme, but the cushion of comedy allows viewers to experience joy rather than horror when characters periodically confess to prison rape, assault, or murder. Laugh tracks are added when punch lines are delivered, creating a strange ambivalence in which viewers feel invited or even obliged to laugh along.[181] In one episode, the incarcerated characters take Charlie and another man hostage during a prison riot, yet even when their lives are all threatened, the humor of the dialogue (along with the laugh track) leaves the audience free from the concern that we are about to be subjected to something shocking or horrific.[182]

The 1996 prison comedy *Life* is a classic example of the penitentiary wrapped in the cushion of comedy.[183] Like *Anger Management*, the film adopts an overtly comical tone, leaving viewers protected by a constant bubble of comfort concerning the subject matter. In one scene, a guard offers Gibson (Eddie Murphy) his freedom if he shoots his friend, Banks (Martin Lawrence), but the comedic tone allows viewers to rest assured that a murder is not about to take place. A perfectly timed joke cements our comfort, and instead of a murder we are treated to Gibson's poke at the guard: "I got to be honest with you boss. You don't want to give me that gun; I'd probably shoot you with it." In a tense scene in *The Shawshank Redemption* when the despondent warden raises a pistol to his head as the authorities close in, the somber atmosphere leaves viewers with no such assurance of safety, and the graphic suicide that ensues is hardly a surprise.[184]

Similarly, during Gibson's famous cornbread diatribe in *Life*, when he responds to a large man's demand for his cornbread with threats of "consequences and repercussions," the cushion of comedy protects viewers from the threat of serious violence, and this protection continues even as a comedic fight scene ensues. A similar scene takes place in *Cool Hand Luke* after Luke questions the authority of the largest man in his camp, leading to a fight that plays out nearly the same as in *Life,* only without the cushion of comedy. Gibson and Luke both refuse to stop fighting even after they are obviously defeated—a shout-out to toxic masculinity which is frequently included in depictions of men's prison environments—but the primary difference between the two fight scenes lies in the framing of the movie up to that point. The cushion of comedy assures audiences that Gibson is not likely to be seriously injured or killed in *Life*, while the somber tone sustained in *Cool Hand Luke* makes it difficult to know how that fight will end. Scenes where comedy is used to defuse otherwise tense situations *look* the same as those without comedic cushioning; but they *feel* different. When applied to the entire script as opposed to just the outlaw, the framework of comedy allows producers to press the limits of prison as a playground into the realm of sadism without triggering the responses we would normally have to human suffering. Burke's comedic framework not only disables our disgust of the prisoner and their crime, but when applied appropriately, it also disables our disgust at the prison environment and the horrible things shown to happen there.

In 2006, *Let's go to Prison!* presented the trope of prison as a playground, heavily cloaked in a cushion of comedy that frequently bordered on slapstick.[185] Producers used humor to explore themes such as drinking wine made in a toilet, violent assault, attempted murder and rape, all while preserving an atmosphere designed to elicit joy rather than sorrow or empathy. A *New York Times* movie review said as much, suggesting that the movie "is actually a sly, very funny comedy, one that stays admirably deadpan every time you think it's about to veer into gross-out territory."[186] That's quite a claim, considering the horrible scenes of victimization depicted throughout the film that seem very much like the heart of "gross-out territory." At one point in the movie, a man sells his roommate to another man, and when the unwitting victim is dragged from his cell by a gang and delivered to his "purchaser," viewers understand that a sexual assault is taking place. However, despite the distasteful subject matter, the following scene is packed with elements designed to elicit laughter from the audience rather than horror: a *Kama Sutra* sex-position poster hangs on the rapist's cell wall; he offers his victim Merlot wine made "in the toilet" to loosen him up; and rather than an actual rape, the scene ends with a harmless kunik—they rub their noses together. In the next scene, the main character is stabbed in the leg with a fork, but his assailant quickly pulls the fork back out and continues to eat his meal with it. The film is packed with similar plotlines depicting cruelty and sexual victimization, yet instead of experiencing guttural disgust, we find ourselves chuckling along, immune to our own natural reactions.

In 2013, Netflix's hit prison drama *Orange is the New Black* began a seven-season run by winning a Peabody Award for excellence in quality storytelling. In 2014 the show was nominated 14 times for Emmy Awards, and it won the award for Outstanding Casting for a Comedy Series. As of this writing, the final season has an impressive 98% rating on the popular cinema review website RottenTomatoes.com. Producers clearly hit on something the public ate up with this series, and the cushion of comedy is a big part of why it works. Even though Litchfield prison, where the series is set, is a far cry from the violence and depravity of Shawshank, Fox River or Oz, the series still requires a cushioning of blows because the characters are women, and as previously discussed, culturally, the violence which we find entertaining as part of male prison cinema isn't as enjoyable when it's inflicted on women's bodies. In a men's prison, when a scene isn't good enough, producers can simply crank up the mayhem, allowing viewers to separate themselves from the spectacle as men's bodies are destroyed for entertainment.[187] But in a women's prison, our patriarchal cultural norms won't allow us to enjoy the abuse of women's bodies or the hyperviolence of savage fights the same way as we can when men are the victims.[188] Instead of avoiding this axiom, Kohan leaned in.

Piper's journey is hilarious from start to finish, and because we are laughing, we don't feel the discomfort of various events that would otherwise make us experience apprehension or empathy. When she arrives at prison to turn herself in, she is asked who she is with, and responds, "my fiancé," to which a guard quips, "Yeah? Good luck with that." When she kisses her partner goodbye, she reminds him to "update my BLOG." When she gets to her cell for the first time, another white girl hands her a bar of soap and a toothbrush, then says, "we look out for our own." When Piper blurts out what the viewer is thinking—"excuse me?"—the girl presses back, "don't get all PC on me. It's tribal, not racist." In each of these scenes, we, as viewers, are suddenly in the middle of an awkward situation. If it wasn't hilarious, we would probably turn it off and watch something else. But we relate because we are laughing, and the cushion of comedy allows us to engage without the risk of becoming offended. After all, it's just a joke.

Regardless of the comedic tone adopted, films and television shows that depict the trope of prison as a playground reinforce the importance and legitimacy of the archetypal obstinate lawman and the prison industrial complex as a whole.[189] Beneath the antics that make us laugh lie truly disturbing patterns of behavior, and despite our willingness to consume the story without cringing, we still understand that the characters are dangerous people who we don't want living in our neighborhood. When prisons are filled with sexual predators, violent criminals, proud tribalists and unrepentant murderers, the obstinate lawman magically transforms into the story's lone hero, whether the cushion of comedy is used or not.[190]

The trope of prison as a playground flips the dynamic of the archetypal outlaw and lawman from *Les Misérables* on its head. This juxtaposition paints the obstinate lawman as society's sole savior, and as the only person who can see through the façade and recognize the rotten apples of society as the irredeemable outlaws they truly are. As Yousman has suggested, "brutalizing fictions" suggest that the current penal system is too easy on those inside, "that rehabilitation is impossible, that prisoners are dangerous creatures who require severe punishment, and that, ultimately, capital punishment is the only solution."[191] But it is *so* fun to watch.

The Fresh Fish Fetish

In the trope of prison as a playground, the cushion of comedy allows viewers to obtain pleasure from otherwise forbidden sources by cloaking the sadistic behavior of characters in a safe, comedic tone. In other prison cinema scenes, producers take advantage of our preexisting knowledge, wrong as it often is, that prison is full of rituals and rules we cannot understand, along with monsters who love to use those rules to their advantage. When straight characters are shown to "turn gay" because of prison, or when dropping the soap is shown to result in sexual assault, or when a candy bar on the new guy's pillow is a trick meant to trap him in an abusive relationship, we know what is going on even though we have no idea what is going on. It doesn't make any sense, but of course, we also believe that prison doesn't make any sense. I'll examine this construction of prison from the victim's perspective in later chapters, where I discuss the trope of prison as a paradox, but for the perpetrator who understands the confusing rules and can use them to victimize others, such representations reinforce the trope of prison as a playground. The dialectical tension between new arrivals and everyone else comes to a head in scenes that depict what I will refer to as the fresh fish fetish.

Fresh fish representations usually begin with new arrivals being herded into a prison, while tenured old-timers threaten and cajole them from nearby. One of the most famous fresh fish scenes is in *The Shawshank Redemption,* when Andy and a group of other new arrivals are unloaded from a transport bus that is surrounded on three sides by rowdy men shaking and banging on the fences that restrain them. Those on the yard greet the newcomers with whistles, cheers, and applause, and the first audible phrase viewers hear is, "Hey fish, come on over here." The situation becomes more volatile as Andy is marched past the cheering throng, and the veterans begin making bets on which fish they can break down first.

Later that night, when the lights turn off and the guards vacate the cellblock, a low, resonating voice sings, "Hey fish! Fish, fish, fishy . . . you ain't scared of dying, is you?" Red (the film's narrator) explains the scene as it unfolds: "The boys always go fishing with first timers, and they don't quit until they reel someone in." Shortly after the catcalls begin, one of the "fish" breaks down and begins to loudly cry out for his mother, as an off-camera voice proclaims, "We have a winner!" The scene comes to a dramatic conclusion with the entire cellblock chanting "Fresh fish! Fresh fish! Fresh fish!" causing the guards to return. The cheers immediately stop when the officers reenter the area, but the silence is broken by the continued whimpering of the despondent man still crying for his mother. When he cannot stop, the guards remove him from his cell and beat him to death with their nightsticks in full view of the rest of the cellblock. Whatever a fish is, it is clearly a disadvantage—one that might well result in one's death.

The Shawshank Redemption depicts the prison environment not only as a physical threat, but also as an emotional and mental threat, a place where it seems that psychological breakdown at the hands of other incarcerated people is a very real danger. As upcoming chapters will reveal, the tropes of prison as penance and prison as a paradox often work hand in hand by positioning scenes of abuse from guards or other incarcerated characters as turning points in an outlaw's life. The result of such storylines is viewers who walk away knowing that prison is an awful place packed with awful people who do awful things without feeling awful about it, but that fortunately, the abuse they dish out can sometimes initiate a change of heart in otherwise stubborn outlaws.

In *Prison Break,* Scofield deals with the fresh fish fetish shortly after he arrives. As he leans on his cell bars, staring out into the larger housing unit, someone across the hallway yells, "Yo fish, what you lookin' at? You look kind of pretty to be up in here."[192] His cellmate offers him some advice at this point: "I suggest you take a seat, fish. There ain't nothing to do up in here but serve time." The scene ends with a man being stabbed just outside their cell, and as the victim cries out in pain, Scofield's cellmate speaks up again: "welcome to prisonleyland, fish." Fish is a label placed on those who are seen as potential victims, on the new guys who have not yet shown themselves capable of surviving inside. Writers for *Prison Break* used the label to ramp up the level of threat aimed at Scofield, and when it becomes his longstanding nickname used by many of his enemies, the urgency surrounding the escape plot is naturally increased, keeping us tuned in.

A similar fresh fish theme is also poignantly presented in *Animal Factory,* a film in which, as *New York Times* columnist

Elvis Mitchell described, "institutional life is treated as quotidian, a norm to which most of the men have already adjusted."[193] In one scene, an old-timer points out the story's redeemed outlaw to another guy on the yard by saying, "The new guy over there . . . he's a fish, but he's alright." The man responds with a sexual inuendo: "Is he a broad?"[194] The underlying theme is that reputation is everything in prison, and that anyone who has been there for long enough to escape the fresh fish stage of incarceration has probably survived by moving on to the victimization of others. The sexually charged response informs viewers that the term fish indicates more than just one's recent arrival, but also implies that one is inexperienced, and therefore a potential victim of the innumerable monsters in the background. *Animal Factory* follows the theme of the fresh fish fetish throughout the movie, as the plot revolves around a young outlaw who is taken under the wing of a veteran and protected from the typical dangers associated with being a fish until he learns how to escape those dangers, in large part by victimizing others.

In another example of the fresh fish fetish, *Blood In Blood Out,* viewers follow outlaw Miklo into San Quentin prison. Roger Ebert described the 1993 release as a brutal film that "shows a prison world where guards and officials essentially stand aside while prison gangs run the institution, distribute favors, make rules, and enforce their laws with violence."[195] The fresh fish trope begins as the transport bus pulls up to the main gate of the prison and a pair of guards on the overhead boardwalk are heard commenting, "Another fish tank in from L.A."[196] The bus enters the gate and drives past an expansive exercise yard packed with hundreds of men who all appear to be lifting weights, and one of them asks another, "What the fuck do we got here? Fucking fresh fish, can you believe this shit?"

The new arrivals exit the bus and the jeers begin immediately, with the majority of sexual innuendos directed at the young Miklo. A large, bearded man with a muscled, shirtless friend yells, "Hey baby! Been a long time since I had a West-Texas ballroom bitch. How about you being my ol' lady?" as his friend grabs his crotch and says "*Mamacita*, look over here. I got something for you!" The jeers don't stop when they enter the cellblock. As Miklo walks to his cell for the first time, an unseen voice shouts, "It smells like fish!" Such presentations create an atmosphere where the newly incarcerated are at a disadvantage inside the prison environment simply because they are new, and the threats frequently transcends vulgar jeers and shouted sexual advances, entering a realm that could be referred to as prison as sadism.

Prison as Sadism

Blood In Blood Out follows the fresh fish fetish beyond the simple use of the pejorative, and as Miklo explores the prison for the first time, he is confronted by a group whose behavior resembles the sexually aggressive actions of The Sisters from *The Shawshank Redemption*. As he passes their table, one of them places a hand on Miklo's chest and says, "*Hola* Pretty, are you blond all over?" Miklo responds angrily and slaps the hand away, but someone else in the group grabs him by the shirt. Before the confrontation can proceed any further, an apparent hero named Popeye notices a gang tattoo on Miklo's hand and intervenes. After he sends the attackers away, Popeye takes Miklo on a brief-yet-harrowing tour of the prison. In less than five minutes, Popeye makes it clear that the entire prison is divided into racial cliques, explaining, "It's the gangs that run this place," the Black Guerilla Army, the Arian Vanguard, and his own primarily Mexican La Onda: "We clique together for power, to protect ourselves." Miklo, who is in prison for the first time, is immediately placed in a setting replete with threats of physical violence and sexual predatory behavior, surrounded by others who all seem to want to fight him, rape him, or both.

As the film progresses, the trope of prison as a playground is taken to extremes usually reserved for representations cushioned by comedy. As he follows his guide through the dayroom, a man who Popeye is indebted to suggests, "Maybe you would like to swap for some of that tender, white meat. You can pay your bets with that," suggesting that fresh fish Miklo can be traded as a sex slave. Once they finally reach Milko's cell, Popeye springs a trap and attacks him with a knife, attempting to rape him. This assault is only halted when the leader of yet another prison gang intervenes. In just his first day in prison, Miklo is roughly accosted by a group of sexual predators, stabbed by a sex-crazed rapist, and introduced to three large prison gangs. Eigenberg and Baro describe the consequences of such portrayal, suggesting that movies that "sensationalize male rape in prison may actually contribute to a social structure that has come to accept, perhaps even endorse, that rape is part and parcel of the incarceration experience."[197] It is hard to imagine how anyone who has lived in an environment as horrific as the trope of prison as sadism could ever readapt to regular public life. It's even harder to want that person living in your neighborhood. Frequent consumption of prison as a playground narratives results in uncritical support for the prison industrial complex.

Blood In Blood Out follows the roadmap of cinematic progress from fresh fish to sexual predator, as Miklo learns to navigate the dangerous prison and becomes a bit of a monster himself; he evolves from the role of victim to that of perpetrator. As viewers, it seems like a natural evolution, given the situation, and we watch as prison turns a young man on the cusp of adulthood into a violent, career criminal. Later in the film, acting on the orders of a prison gang leader, Miklo lures a man into a storage room with an offer of oral sex, only to spring a trap and brutally stab him to death, signifying his graduation from fresh fish to experienced victimizer. The constant barrage of graphic violence and sexual assault, frequently directed at new arrivals from nearly everyone in the prison, makes it seem as if these activities are a normal part of the incarceration experience. The prison industrial complex thrives on cinematic depictions of mayhem inside prison; viewers expect some amount of truth to be represented on screen, even when they know the story is made up.

Blood In Blood Out, along with an entire genre of *Oz*-like prison movies that depict the behavior of those in prison as sadistic and unrepentant, transcend the trope of prison as a playground and enter the realm of prison as sadism. Rather than exposing the bad behavior of the few, fresh fish representations suggest that *everyone* who goes to prison is likely to be subjected to confusing and dangerous situations in which sadistic predators will take advantage of them, often for no discernable reason. The only way for fish to prevent the abuse they are certain to sustain at the hands of their tormentor(s) is to become a tormentor themselves—to make prison into their own evil playground.

Oz is perhaps the best-known contemporary example of prison as sadism.[198] It still holds a 98% audience score rating on RottenTomatoes.com two decades after its conclusion, largely because it raised the bar on hyperviolent spectacles of incarceration. In six seasons, from 1997 – 2003, *Oz* told stories about people in prison up to all sorts of macabre behavior: grinding up glass and feeding it to others, lighting one another on fire, participating in riots, and even building a wall at one point to encase a still-living character in a permanent tomb, with plenty of murder and sexual assault to fill in the gaps. *Oz* was designed to present an image of the worst of the worst in criminals. The show is set in a maximum-security housing unit which originated as an experiment in managing the most dangerous men in custody, including a cannibal, a leader of the Aryan Brotherhood, a man who executed a police officer by chopping off his head, and countless other wicked characters whose crimes are often described in lurid detail during episode introductions.

Perhaps the oddest thing about *Oz*'s over-the-top script is that it tends to strike viewers as realistic. As Erica Meiners has suggested, it offers "audiences the feeling and belief that they know what life is like in a maximum security institution" despite its obvious intent to present stories so intense and exaggerated that few would actually accept them as truth had they come from someone they know.[199] Despite its exaggerated plotlines and over-the-top violence, we walk away from episodes of *Oz* feeling as if we have experienced an actual prison environment. Such cinematic accounts of prison are vital in the maintenance of our cultural disdain for those who wind up in prison. Frequent viewing of *Oz*-like worlds leaves viewers with a skewed perception of life behind bars and a warped opinion of the people who occupy prisons. We forget how expensive it is to lock someone up and how traumatic it is to experience incarceration because we already feel as if we know a lot about those in prison, in large part because we have spent so much time with them on TV.

Our bad media diet leaves us viewing those in prison as depraved monsters who require increasingly harsh punishment if they are to be contained. Whether the representations are brutally sadistic or cloaked in the cushion of comedy, cinematic accounts of the spectacle of punishment (including representations of prison as a playground) reinforce society's belief that massive correctional institutions and increasingly severe criminal sanctions are a vital part of a well-managed and growing social apparatus. In the end, we come to support the continued expansion and harshening of the prison industrial complex.

Prison is a playground for some. But it's not like in the movies. It isn't organized crime or rampant sexual assaults which go unpunished. It's more like ingenuity in the face of adversity—the art of what Tupac often described as growing roses from concrete.[200] There are people who can look past the dull, grey drab and the torturous monotony of prison to find spaces in the margins for making a profit or creating something beautiful. Of course, self-employment is against the rules in prison. You are allowed to work for the state (you're actually required to do so), but you can't work for yourself because no trading of property or currency is allowed between incarcerated people.

But that doesn't mean it doesn't happen.

The store guy is the most obvious example. When you show up to a prison, sometimes your money doesn't show up with you, and you wind up waiting on it to purchase items you need, like snacks, soap or toothpaste. The store guy can help, but he will charge you a little extra in repayment for whatever you need now. Since cash is against the rules, as is exchanging goods with others, you can pay him in bars of soap or bags of Ramon Noodle Soup to prevent detection.

There are plenty of other services for sale in prison. You can have your clothes ironed, even though most prisons don't have an iron for general use. You can also pay to have your clothes washed by hand if you don't want them mixed in with the weekly institutional soup from everyone else's dirty laundry. There are guys who can fix your TV if it's broken (even though soldering irons aren't allowed), guys who can draw you a custom card for your kid's birthday (or a dirty picture if you prefer), and even guys who can type up a letter for you, or draft court documents.

My favorite hustle was the cook. There are all sorts of clever ways people use the elements at their disposal to create something delicious. Large pots or bowls were not available in the prisons where I was locked up. To accommodate a meal made to share with a dozen or so people, the cook would often construct his master-piece in a garbage bag, then cut the bottom corner out to dispense the final product, like frosting a cake with a pastry bag. On special occasions, our cook would fry up sandwiches by scraping the paint off his bunk and heating it from below with a rigged-up burner.

Some people write books while in prison. Others create and publish beautiful works of art, poetry, prose and even research. Many of my students spend their time inside earning college cred-its or high school diplomas. For others, the goal becomes spiritual exploration and awakening. Their efforts are impressive in the face of an experience that often requires every bit of one's will simply to survive (or to want to).

For most of those who wind up there, prison is boredom and monotony; it's tedious banality of the worst sort. But for those who can find a niche and carve out an identity, a small piece of it becomes a kind of playground—a place where one can find some solace from the stress of daily existence. Unfortunately, Hollywood neglects this sort of portrayal in favor of prisons packed with mon-sters and plots driven by mayhem and murder.

Chapter 6

Prison as Penance

"Carceral visibility makes incarcerated people both invisible and hypervisible, but also unseeing and unseen. Public life generally excluded incarcerated people, but their shadow presence and status as the punished are the foundational components to the perception of freedom, access and mobility in the United States."[201]
—*Nicole Fleetwood*

"In societies where modern conditions of production prevail, all of life presents itself as an immense accumulation of spectacles. Everything that was directly lived has moved away into a representation . . . the spectacle is not a collection of images, but a social relation among people, mediated by images."[202] —*Guy Debord*

The trope of prison as a playground is not the only show in town. While it appears the most often in prison cinema, it is frequently depicted alongside its counterparts, prison as penance and prison as a paradox. The trope of prison as penance, the focus of this chapter, paints the penitentiary as a dangerous-yet-necessary warehouse for society's recalcitrant rule-breakers. Such cinematic representations reveal a correctional system that is ultimately successful in either containing bad people who refuse to be reformed, or in eliminating the criminality of those who are redeemable, although they might experience trauma in the process. In dealing with the creepy villains Hollywood dreams up, representations of prison as penance depict the penitentiary as serving a valuable purpose—providing the justified punishment required to keep the public safe. By filling the prison with guilty-yet-unrepentant characters, many who seem incapable of ever being reformed, the trope of prison as penance emphasizes the necessity of prison as a tool of social order. Prison as penance is obvious in stories where the outlaw finally finds a way to live a better life by giving up criminality, usually as a direct result of things experienced during incarceration. But it also manifests in depictions of prison as a space where those who can never be reformed go to serve out their punishment in the protection of the public, and ultimately, to die at the hands of the system.

As we have already seen, bestselling author Stephen King has proven especially adept in the creation of fictional prison narratives which translate well to film. In a *Chicago Tribune* article, journalist Julia Keller praised King's uncanny "ability to create, time and again, stories that adhere themselves to the inside of the reader's mind like some vicious, twisted Velcro."[203] In 1995, King teamed up with director Frank Darabont to create a film version of *The Shawshank Redemption.* The previous chapter unpacked the various ways in which that film shocked audiences with the trope of prison as a playground, represented by "The Sisters," a dirty warden, and a host of compromised guards willing to do anything for a buck.

King's success stems in part from the fact that he does not restrict his prison representations to a single trope. In *The Shawshank Redemption,* audiences also get a dose of the trope of prison as penance in the film's narrator, Red. As the movie unfolds, a theme emerges in which nearly everyone in Shawshank seems unwilling to admit their guilt. Red exposes this prison film norm when he asks the story's redeemed outlaw, Andy, why he killed his wife, and Andy responds by claiming he is innocent. Red reacts with a chuckle, "You are going to fit right in. Everyone in here is innocent, you know that?" He then yells to another man across the yard, "Hayward, what you in here for?" and is rewarded with the response, "I'm innocent. My lawyer fucked me."

This snippet of dialogue highlights the necessity of Shawshank Prison's objective punitive stance: everyone sent to Shawshank must receive the same harsh treatment and be required to follow the same regimen, regardless of any subjective circumstances (such as professed innocence). The trope of prison as penance requires the penitentiary to be a machine of punishment, and this machine must operate with equal objectivity on each of its charges. Like its faithful partner, the obstinate lawman, the prison industrial complex lacks the capacity for recognizing innocence or redemption in individual outlaws. Prison is hard and cold, but in cinematic representations of prison as penance, it is ultimately effective in protecting society from the dangers of unrepentant villains who won't so much as admit their guilt.

A portrayal of an entire prison packed with criminals who all refuse to take responsibility, and by proxy, to recognize the legitimacy of the punitive sanctions placed upon them, cunningly advocates for the necessity of the prison industrial complex as a way to punish and contain recalcitrant, dangerous criminals. If the outlaw won't take responsibility, they can never begin to seek true redemption for their crimes, and the viewer is off the hook for accepting harsh punishments we might otherwise be forced to rethink.[204] The universal feigned innocence claimed by nearly every character in *The Shawshank Redemption* leaves guards and prison officials with no option except to disregard every outlaw's individuality, and to instead assume that everyone in prison is the same: guilty, dishonest and intractably unrepentant.

Red is the sole exception to the norm of denial in Shawshank. He readily admits his guilt to the viewer, to the parole board, and even to those incarcerated with him, at one point joking that he is the "only guilty man in Shawshank." He also expresses sincere regret for his crimes, not just for being caught, lamenting at one point that "there's not a day goes by that I don't feel regret . . . I look back on the way I was—a young, stupid kid who committed a terrible crime—and I wanna talk to him, talk some sense into him." With his confession, Red positions himself as a redeemed outlaw by accepting his guilt and expressing a desire to be a different person than he once was; he separates himself from the ranks of the majority, who continue to stubbornly profess their innocence.[205] When the redeemed outlaw is found to be different than his cohort—when one of the multitude decrying their false convictions is found to be telling the truth—the obstinate lawman breaks down, as seen in Javert's suicide, the warden from *Escape from Alcatraz* who denies that the escapees survived, the parole board at Shawshank who won't accept anyone's claims of redemption, and an endless list of other films which deploy the same trope.

The obstinate lawman lacks the ability to expect or to recognize anything other than stereotypical criminal behavior in the outlaw. This lack of flexibility is seen in another scene in *The Shawshank Redemption,* when a new arrival to the prison reveals evidence to the warden that will likely result in the acquittal of the main outlaw. Instead of turning it in, the warden locks Andy in solitary confinement for sixty days while he has the witness murdered. The trope of prison as penance lacks the space for false convictions and mistakes in the system. When they arise, they are quickly covered up.

King and Darabont teamed up again in 1999 with *The Green Mile,* a film that Roger Ebert called, "Dickensian."[206] King built the story around the epitome of penance: the death penalty. *The Green Mile*'s redeemed outlaw is John Coffey, an aboding man who is much taller than everyone else around him, but who comes across as unthreatening based on his soft demeanor and low speech. He is also innocent, as we discover early into the story, falsely convicted of a crime he attempted to prevent. The obstinate lawman is Officer Percy Wetmore, a prison guard who obtained his job on death row from his uncle, the governor. Throughout the film, Wetmore consistently abuses and even tortures those he is paid to guard: he intentionally breaks one man's fingers with his nightstick, he crushes another man's pet mouse, and he causes yet another to painfully burn to death during an official execution. His sadistic behavior is always aimed at a character who is sentenced to death, and he clearly draws a distinction between his fellow officers, whom he typically treats with obligatory respect, and those he is paid to watch over, whom he mercilessly torments. If punishment of the worst sort is what you are trying to dream up, Wetmore is the guard you want.

In the trope of prison as a playground, the bad behavior of those in prison is aimed at some sort of incentive; the Sisters at Shawshank want sex, Schofield and T-Bag want to escape, and the characters in *Oz* are typically seeking drugs, sex, money, or power. But Wetmore's cruelty is coldly disconnected from any sort of palpable reward. Instead, he appears to obtain pleasure simply from inflicting physical and psychological pain on people in prison. Even Wetmore's assignment to death row suggests a morbid predisposition, for his nepotistic ties allowed him any job in the state, yet he chose the one that was sure to expose him to suffering and death. This ambiguity of motives leaves viewers with the impression that Wetmore is a demented sadist who revels in the agony of others, and as such, perhaps a death house cellblock is the best place for him; otherwise, he may release his sinister impulses on society. In upcoming chapters, I will examine the paradox presented by a guard who appears to enjoy torturing people for no discernable reason, but in the context of prison as penance, characters like Wetmore—sadists who make the already terrifying atmosphere of prison even more chilling—also work to ramp up the atonement heaped upon those he is charged with guarding. His brand of punishment transcends death by adding the indignity of torture.

The Green Mile also centers the necessity of prison as penance through "Wild" Bill Wharton, a character who consistently manipulates the guards and his fellow incarcerated neighbors to instigate excitement in the otherwise dull environment. Wharton enters the story as a new arrival, although he is far from a fish. He pretends to be overmedicated during his transport only to spring an assault on the unsuspecting guards as soon as they arrive in the cellblock. But he isn't trying to escape; he is trying to have fun. Wharton stubbornly revels in the system that will eventually take his life, consistently creating chaos and celebration in the otherwise calm environment. He insults others who are in prison with him. He cracks jokes as if he doesn't have a care in the world. When the lights dim one night during an execution, he screams and swings wildly from the bars of his cell, loudly banging on the walls and chanting, "He's frying now!"

Wharton is an unrepentant villain who appears beyond rehabilitation. Even the most extreme form of punishment available—death—isn't enough to make this outlaw change his ways. As viewers, we are treated to yet another rendition of an irredeemable monster barely contained by an indispensable system. Luckily, we know he is already where he belongs—in a place where he can't hurt us. Prison as penance thrives when the outlaw is incapable of rehabilitation and the prison is constructed as a crucial part of a functioning society, a necessary device vital to keeping those evil others away from the rest of us until they die. The characters in these dramas are more than just prisoners; they play a vital role in the construction of prison as a character, for without them the penitentiary would be nothing more than an empty zoo.

Torture as Punishment

The trope of prison as penance works even when the punishment that appears to instigate change in the outlaw is so extreme it might better be called torture. In *American History X,* redeemed outlaw Derek Vinyard murders a young, black man who he catches breaking into his car, and his subsequent trip to prison is framed as justified punishment for his racially motivated crime. Once Vinyard gets to prison, the atmosphere rapidly evolves from a simple depiction of prison as penance to an extreme example of prison as torture, with a side of prison as a playground. In a pivotal scene that exemplifies this shift, Vinyard is gang raped by his fellow white supremacists in retaliation for befriending a black man, depicting playground (sadism) for the assaulters. The brutal attack, which, for Vinyard, represents prison as torture (penance), becomes a central piece of his story. It causes him to reevaluate, and to eventually discard his prior racist belief system.

While the concept of justified punishment (for murder) provides the basis for Vinyard's incarceration, as Eigenberg and Baro posit, "*American History X* also uses rape as a central theme to motivate major change in the main character," and it is clear to viewers that the rape, rather than his incarceration, causes Vinyard to become disillusioned with his radical views.[207] The torture he experiences at the hands of the system and those who operate as part of it works to transform him from a bad guy into a good guy. His penance, although brutal, is ultimately shown to be useful in instigating change. The single violent gang rape appears to have been *more effective* than the entire prison sentence Vinyard had served up to that point. Until he was raped, Vinyard had never so much as questioned his principles. The assault instigated a vital change of heart.

Rather than pure disgust and abhorrence, viewers of *American History X* must consider whether the sexual assault Vinyard sustained was, in the end, a *good thing*, for it seems to have initiated a drastic update in his values. Even if we reject the notion that rape and the threat of rape constitute a legitimate component of the criminal justice system or an effective form of rehabilitation, we are still left with the impression that gang rape in prison is a regular occurrence, that those in prison are often rapists, and that keeping those people behind bars is a good idea.[208] When cinematic prisons are packed with violent, unrepentant monsters victimizing one another without punishment, the necessity of the prison industrial complex is tacitly reinforced. When the trope of prison as penance is constructed by abuse sustained at the hands of others who are also incarcerated, viewers come to see prison as an environment where victimizers are as much a part of the punishment machine as the guards.

Other films are even more explicit in their utilization of incarcerated characters to achieve what appears to be impossible through official means. In 1977, *Short Eyes* told the fictional story of Clark Davis, a man who finds himself in jail awaiting trial on charges of raping a little girl.[209] *The New York Times* said that the story's main character stands out "as the victim of victims, but also because he gives a performance so intimate it's almost painful to watch."[210] In the film, Davis tells his cellmate that he does not remember the crime he is accused of committing, but he admits that he has perpetrated a number of similar crimes against children in the past—offenses that were never brought to the attention of authorities. In a macabre twist of the trope of prison as penance,

Davis is likely to be released based on shoddy evidence, but those in jail with him (the film's stand in archetypal obstinate lawmen) take matters into their own hands and mete out an arbitrary sentence of death. In a gruesome finale, Davis is bound and placed on top of a table in the middle of the cellblock. Despite his pleas for mercy, his throat is cut from ear to ear, and he bleeds to death as his killers stand by watching.

Much like *American History X*'s depiction of rape as a valuable tool of punishment, viewers of *Short Eyes* must consider which is the lesser of two evils—releasing an unrepentant child molester back into the community to (presumably) reoffend, or endorsing the brutal, unsanctioned execution of a man who has been convicted of no crime. As seen in both *American History X* and *Short Eyes,* the trope of prison as penance can leave audience members with a sense that sexual violence and murder are acceptable methods of punishment, or at the very least, extreme options for especially difficult cases. Once again, even if we reject the notion that sometimes torture is an effective way to change someone's heart, or to prevent them from hurting future victims, we still come to accept the idea that murder and rape are common occurrences in prison, and that prisons are packed with active, unrepentant rapists and murderers—those ghastly monsters we don't want living next door to us.

The concept of the imprisoned coming to act as substitute lawmen who are ready to step in when the official lawman is unable to adequately perform their duty has also been adapted to numerous other prison narratives, some of which present the redeemed outlaw as such a likeable and trustworthy character that he seems to slip seamlessly into the role of auxiliary lawman. One such movie, *Con Air,* tells the story of Cameron Poe (Nicolas Cage), an archetypal redeemed outlaw who audiences from patriarchal cultures immediately sympathizes with because his crime was a justifiable homicide committed in part to protect a woman.[211] *The New York Times* film critic Janet Maslin described the main character's likability as follows: "Cameron Poe: he's our hero . . . he loves his family. He protects women. He sounds like Elvis . . . He must be a really nice guy."[212]

In *Con Air*, Poe returns home from war a decorated veteran, but when three men attack his pregnant wife and him one night as they leave a restaurant, he accidentally kills one of the attackers in self-defense. A conviction of involuntary manslaughter lands him in prison for seven years, where he finds himself surrounded by a group of characters who exemplify the trope of prison as a playground. But Poe himself reflects the trope of prison as penance. His calm demeanor assures viewers he poses no danger to society, and that the only reason he is in prison is to serve out his punishment. We don't expect Poe to exhibit a change of heart or to embrace a more benevolent belief system, for he simply defended his wife when they were attacked, an action that demands no redemption to our Western eyes. Although he did commit the crime he is accused of, viewers sympathize with him for the same reason that we feel sorry for Andy in *The Shawshank Redemption*, or Carl Lee Hailey in *A Time to Kill*; despite their apparent "guilt," both characters are victims of circumstances beyond their control.[213]

Con Air unfolds as a group of violent prisoners, along with the soon-to-be-paroled Poe, are loaded aboard a prison transport airplane. Unbeknownst to most of those onboard, an escape plan is already in motion. Shortly after takeoff, the bad guys, who know nothing of Poe's recently granted parole, overtake the guards and seize control of the plane. The obstinate lawman in *Con Air* is US Marshall Vince Larkin (John Cusack), who is dedicated to hunting down and recapturing the escapees at any cost. In an unusual plot twist, Poe and Larkin (the outlaw and the lawman) end up working together to catch the rest of the escapees, who are described at one point in the film as, "the worst of the worst . . . these guys are pure predators, each and every one of them." In the end, Poe, our representative of the trope of prison as penance, overcomes the multitude of men who represent the trope of prison as a playground, and we witness our redeemed outlaw separate himself from the villains who surrounded him in prison. As usual, when even the incarcerated are unwilling to offer redemption to one of their own, viewers are invited to follow suit.[214]

In 1993, the previously mentioned *Blood In Blood Out* told the story of redeemed outlaw Paco, a young gang member who signs up for the military to avoid being sent to San Quentin Prison with his friend after they are both involved in the shooting of a local rival gang. The film's obstinate lawman is also Paco; writers managed to position him later in life as a detective in charge of tracking down and arresting his friend, Miklo. The film becomes a "what would have happened if he hadn't redeemed himself" story, as the paths of two friends split, one toward redemption and the other toward recidivism. In one dramatic scene, Paco, working as a police officer, shoots Miklo during an attempted robbery when he tries to escape. The injury leads to the amputation of Miklo's leg, and he is subsequently returned to San Quentin to serve yet another prison sentence as punishment for his continued failures at redemption. Of course, Miklo encounters all sorts of barriers to his success which cause viewers to understand why he eventually gives in to the temptation to embrace criminality and keep committing crimes. But he loses our support when he finally discards the idea of redemption altogether, remaining in prison and rising through the ranks of a national gang. Meanwhile, his friend, who was also a gang member at the beginning of the film, achieves his redemption, in part by returning the irredeemable bad guy to prison.

Miklo presents an excellent example of an archetypal redeemed outlaw who is unwilling or unable to fully embrace the concept of redemption, and his recidivism prevents us from feeling overly sympathetic to his plight, which is seen as a result of his continued bad behavior. Outlaws who stop seeking redemption still aid in the creation of the trope of prison as penance. Since Miklo is guilty of numerous crimes and unwilling to change his behavior, we wind up feeling like an inescapable prison might be the best place for him. Prison as penance reveals a system that is occasionally ineffective at rehabilitation, yet nonetheless vital to public safety as a receptacle for monsters and ghouls who might otherwise victimize the public. And for the especially troublesome outlaw who will stop at nothing to destroy public order, *Blood In Blood Out* introduced viewers to an archetypal prisoner who serves as the ultimate example of prison as penance, the Dead Man Walking.

Chapter 7

Dead Man Walking

"The social origins of crime, and the social and political choices surrounding the use of the death penalty, are said to disappear in these films which present individualised narratives of guilt, innocence and dessert."[215] —*Sean O'Sullivan*

"the historical and rhetorical strength of the different representations of the prisoner that merged historically continues to maintain rhetorical influence in the present."[216] —*John Sloop*

The idea of the death penalty as the ultimate punishment is well tread ground in film, and I have already touched on the importance of such representations, including *The Last Mile, Castle on the Hudson* and *The Green Mile*. The trope of prison as penance reaches its crescendo in Dead Man Walking scenes, which take us to the extreme limits of what the punitive machine can take from those who refuse to acquiesce. In *Blood In Blood Out*, the prison setting is portrayed as a dangerous spectacle dominated by the threat of physical violence and sexual assault: the trope of prison as a playground. But since the story's main incarcerated character (Miklo) is patently guilty of numerous crimes, and since he is surrounded by violent villains yet seems to fit right in, viewers get the sense that such punitive prisons are necessary institutions of righteous punishment and threat containment. Where else can you put someone like Milko?

Representations of prison as a playground often include scenes where incarcerated characters (along with viewers) are reminded of additional potential punishment—of what can ultimately be taken from them if they don't straighten up and begin seeking redemption. In one representative scene in *Blood In Blood Out*, Miklo is being shown around the recreation yard when two guards appear, one escorting a shackled man while the other repeatedly announces, "Dead man walking." The man on death row plays no further role in the movie. He is included simply to highlight the punitive nature of the prison setting, and to symbolize the ability of the prison industrial complex to procure, if necessary, the ultimate payback through the taking of a life as punishment for a crime. Such representations suggest that the character of the Dead Man Walking is as much a necessary part of the prison industrial complex as any other. The death penalty is the natural end point of a punitive philosophy based on the trope of prison as penance, always looming in the background waiting to do the work that the lawman can't finish in especially difficult cases.

In *The Shawshank Redemption*, the theme of death as penance is emphasized in Red's infamous statement, "they send you here for life, and that's exactly what they take." Although *The Shawshank Redemption* does not include any scenes depicting Dead Men Walking inside the prison, the producers manage to conjure the theme of a system capable of exacting the ultimate penance in the actions of Brooks, when he is released on parole. Brooks has been in prison most of his life, so he struggles to adapt to life outside when he is released. Despondent at his institutionalization, he writes a long letter to his still-incarcerated friends and then takes his own life, demonstrating the inescapable power of prison as penance to exact the ultimate punishment even from those who appear to have escaped its walls. In constructions of prison as penance, the death of the Dead Man Walking need not be official or legislated, nor even to occur in prison; it only need stem from the outlaw's experience with the system. The further away one is when the death takes place, the more powerful and inescapable the prison is ultimately shown to be.

Brooks shows no emotion as he composes his goodbye letter and then hangs himself; he seems to accept the ending as fate. His friends in prison, although saddened, are not at all surprised when they learn what has happened. It appears that Brooks's death was a forgone conclusion, one which Red even foreshadowed in an earlier scene: "the man's institutionalized. This place is all he knows." Such casual acceptance of a character's death invites viewers to feel the same way, as if such an end is just the natural culmination of a life squandered behind bars. Representations depicting so-called "institutionalization," a misunderstood concept which I will unpack in later chapters, remind viewers that even characters like Brooks—a good-hearted, soft-spoken man in his golden years who maintains the prison library prior to his release—can't shake the damage done from incarceration. Perhaps we are lucky he turned his destructive tendencies inward, given his behavior prior to release, when he nearly killed one of his friends in a desperate attempt to remain in prison.

Other films have been even more poignant in depicting outlaws who accept or embrace their eventual fate at the hands of the prison system, leading up to and including state ordered execution. Take, for example, *Monster's Ball*, a film praised by *The New York Times* as "one of those rare movies in which even people glimpsed only for a moment or two seem to have lives that ramify beyond the screen."[217] The film's redeemed outlaw is Lawrence Musgrove (Sean Combs), a Dead Man Walking serving his final days on death row. Musgrove seeks redemption through selfless acts aimed at helping his family prepare for his death. He attempts to earn something like redemption through closure. In one particularly emotional scene, Musgrove is shown saying goodbye just before his execution, and when his adolescent son asks, "I'm not going to see you again after this? Why not?" Musgrove responds, "Because I'm a bad man . . . but you know something? You ain't me."[218] His final words to his wife are, "For every time I hurt you, I'm sorry," and with that, he silently walks away for the last time. Musgrove's ability to face his circumstances with calm acceptance presents a picture of prison in which even those awaiting execution are amicable to the system which orders their death.[219] It's all just business as usual in depictions of the Dead Man Walking. As viewers, we can't very well argue with a character who is calmly embracing their own fate, and so, once again, we are invited to play along, accepting the outcome as natural; that's just the way things are.

A similar scene plays out in *The Last Mile,* when a man who spends the entire film terrified of his own approaching death warrant calmy walks to his execution the day it finally arrives, bragging about how he isn't scared at all anymore.[220] Contrasted with weeks of lamentations leading up to that day, his change of heart reveals that even though the Dead Man Walking might not want to die, he has often accepted the inevitability of his situation. When asked if he has any last words, Musgroves from *Monster's Ball* simply says, "push the button." As he walks to his death, one outlaw in *The Last Mile* quips, "here's to the old death house, boys . . . so long everybody." In *Castle on the Hudson,* the outlaw solemnly walks "the last mile" with the warden, silently accepting the ultimate punishment for a murder he did not commit. In *The Green Mile,* Coffey passes up an opportunity to escape and is ultimately executed despite his innocence. Such cinematic portrayals of state-ordered killing accepted or even endorsed by the person being killed legitimize the trope of prison as penance. When even the character who is sentenced to death feels that their punishment is necessary and deserved, the viewer is left to either join their side, or to stand alone against them.

In *Con Air*, the Dead Man Walking is Cyrus "The Virus" Grissom (John Malkovich), a character whose personality stands in stark contrast to the calm acquiescence of Musgrove from *Monster's Ball*. Cyrus is one of the "worst of the worst," so feared that he is chained up and locked in an individual cage onboard a prison transport plane. His convictions include kidnapping, robbery, extortion, escape, inciting a riot, plus eleven murders committed in prison. At one point the film's obstinate lawman says of him, "He likes to brag that he has killed more men than cancer. Cyrus is a poster child for the criminally insane, a true product of the system."[221] He is surrounded by similarly evil villains, including "Johnny 23" (Danny Trejo), a proud rapist whose name refers to 23 convictions for sexual assault, a number which he claims is inaccurately low.

Where the redeemed outlaw in *Monster's Ball* exhibits a submissive and regretful acceptance of his fate, Cyrus and much of the supporting cast in *Con Air* represent Musgrove's rebellious counterpart. After the guards are overpowered and Cyrus assumes control of the plane, various gratuitous violent assaults and murders follow. As viewers, we see a drastic difference between the enforced calm maintained by the system and the violent chaos that inevitably ensues the second the incarcerated seize control of the situation. The monsters in *Con Air* remind viewers why the death penalty is so important, for even the strictest lockdown possible—chained, caged and supervised by armed guards—isn't enough to prevent some outlaws from committing additional heinous crimes. When we consume these narratives, of course we come to believe that those in prison are irredeemable and dangerous, always on the verge of hatching some sort of dastardly plot to upset the social order.[222] Driving that point home, in the end of *Con Air*, Cameron evolves from the role of redeemed outlaw to that of stand in lawman when he finishes the job which the prison cannot, killing Cyrus and his remaining henchmen.

In *The Green Mile*, the Dead Man Walking theme informs the actions of the sadistic lawman (Wetmore) when he walks the newly arrived John Coffey down the hallway chanting, "Dead man walking. We got a dead man walking here." Since the film is set on death row, Wetmore frequently acts as the embodiment of prison as penance, tormenting and abusing those he is paid to supervise. In a scene that exemplifies his desire to see as much punishment as possible handed out, Wetmore intentionally fails to wet the sponge that is normally placed atop one's head during electrocution to ensure a swift death. His prank causes the killing to take much longer than normal, and for more than three minutes the tortured man flails and struggles against his restraints, only dying after he finally catches on fire. Wetmore seems disgusted at the result of his actions, but when he tries to avert his eyes from the spectacle, his superior officer forces him to watch the horrible death he has caused. In so doing, his fellow guard deploys the trope of prison as penance back onto the lawman, a move that confronts viewers with the possibility that even those who work for the prison are frequently disgusted when forced to witness the results of their own actions.

The three-minute electrocution scene is the most brutal execution depicted in *The Green Mile*, but two additional state-ordered deaths warrants are carried out during the movie. Each time someone is to be executed, a trustee first acts as a stand-in while the staff repetitively walks through the execution from start to finish, to practice. This repeated exposure to the process leading up to a state-ordered death makes it seem casual and ordinary, as if killing someone is just another cog in the expansive machine of justice, no more significant than any other. Driving this business-as-usual trope home, at one point during an execution rehearsal, the guards begin to uncontrollably laugh at a dirty joke the stand-in tells, failing to maintain their composure as they prepare to put a man to death.[223] Death is just part of the job, nothing all that special. Such scenes reinforce the belief that prisons are full of individuals who are destined to the same eventual fate—death at the hands of a system that sees their execution as no big deal.

The cushion of comedy is only one form of situational buffer used to offset our guttural disgust at content we might otherwise reject. In her book, *A Report on the Banality of Evil: Eichmann in Jerusalem,* Hannah Arendt unpacks the groupthink of Nazi Colonel Eichmann and his fellow commanders, who organized and participated in the atrocities of the Holocaust. In trying to understand their unconscionable behavior, Arendt concludes that, "the trouble with Eichmann was precisely that so many were like him, and that the many were neither perverted nor sadistic, that they were, and still are, terribly and terrifyingly normal."[224] In surrounding himself with individuals who were devoted supporters of the Nazi regime, Eichmann committed "crimes under circumstances that make it well nigh impossible for him to know or to feel that he is doing wrong."[225] Eichmann and his men claimed they were just following orders, and they questioned neither the motives nor the integrity of their superiors. In Arendt's analysis, this was not because they were bad people. It was because they were *people.* Groupthink is an unavoidable part of being human. When we find ourselves surrounded by others who endorse an activity, our critical reasoning is deactivated, and what would normally shock us instead becomes palatable, or even acceptable.

A similar effect is utilized by clever producers of prison films. Joking at the banality of their task as they prepare to put someone to death, the guards in *The Green Mile* are simply carrying out the orders of their superiors with indifference, supported by the similar loyalty of their cohort. As viewers, we also find our senses dulled through the casual demeanor of those in charge. This theme reappears in prison cinema of all sorts, from prison as a playground representations of prison gangs and dirty guards, to prison as penance scenes where characters step in to complete the punishment which official systems appear unable to achieve, like in *Short Eyes* and *Con Air*. Any time someone in a prison film is doing something that sickens the spirit and twists the gut, they are likely to be surrounded by a group of supporters, reminding them (and us) that perhaps the behavior in question isn't as bad as we first thought, since so many others support it.

Arendt's business-as-usual theme, exemplified by the trope of the Dead Man Walking, is explored in Tim Robbins's film by the same name, *Dead Man Walking*. The film follows Matthew Poncelet through the months leading up to his execution for murder and rape, and the prison guards are consistently depicted as unemotional participants who are simply performing their official duty, as a team.[226] In Matthew's final visit with his family, which is conducted in a small room as six guards silently stand around the perimeter, a camera shot out the window reveals another group of guards walking one of their own in circles, practicing the proper way to escort Matthew to his death. As his final visit ends, the same guards enter the room and take up the same positions they practiced outside, only this time around Matthew. One of them firmly orders, "Up on your feet," and another coldly tells the family, "You can say your goodbyes now." The guards in the room, now numbering nearly a dozen, are emotionless, unfazed, and authoritative, and their composure remains even as they force Matthew to bid a final farewell. In any other setting, a gang of armed men who force someone to say goodbye to his family before they kill him would appear to be heartless, but thanks to the magic of prison as penance, these men are just doing their job. Shortly after Matthew returns to his cell, the warden coldly informs him that the federal appeals court—his final hope for survival—has turned him down, further illustrating the indifference required to act out the official duties associated with state-ordered executions. We learn over and over from television and film that capital punishment is just the way things are, a required component of any working correctional machine. The plots are just footnotes in the construction of Hollywood outlaws and lawmen. We might feel bad for the Dead Man Walking, but we certainly don't blame the guards or the system for their fate. They are, after all, just doing their jobs.

In the conclusion of *Dead Man Walking,* the machine of justice, indifferent in its execution, is ultimately shown to be effective when Matthew finally gives in and confesses his guilt at the proverbial eleventh hour. Just before he is taken to the execution room, Matthew tells his religious advisor that he was much more involved in the crimes than he previously admitted. As he confesses, a flashback scene depicts a brutal rape and murder committed at the hands of an evil man, providing justification for the execution that is about to occur.

In placing the confession directly before the execution, *Dead Man Walking* portrays the death penalty not only as an effective and necessary tool of justice, but also as a legitimate method of eliciting a confession. We feel better about Matthew's death knowing he is guilty; *for a second there I was worried we were executing an innocent man.* This sort of death sentence serves the dual purpose of punishment and validation—punishment by way of death, and validation of the system by way of eliciting a confession that seemed unobtainable via any other method. This strange cinematic construction of an effective, punitive machine of justice further endorses the belief that the prison industrial complex, and its ultimate tool of penance, capital punishment, are vital instruments for ensuring social order. They might not be perfect, but they forced Matthew to confess when nothing else could, providing closure for the victim's family members as well as for viewers.

As this examination of the trope of prison as penance has shown, cinematic representations that paint the prison environment as a necessary tool of justice reinforce the belief that incarcerated people are recalcitrant, irredeemable monsters who must be punished and contained for the greater good of society. When that punishment is at the hands of others who are also incarcerated rather than prison officials, the trope of prison as penance takes a dangerous turn into cloudy waters where gang rape and group murder appear to be acceptable means to an end. At the far end of the punitive spectrum, the procuring of the ultimate punishment, death, is the most extreme example of the trope of prison as penance. When execution is shown to serve the dual purposes of punishment *and* closure through a last-minute confession that seems to be elicited by the imminent imposition of the sentence, the punitive machine is yet again glorified and shown to be effective.

Prison is penance. It is punishment of the dullest sort. I was punished for being born into an addicted body. For others, it's mental health issues driving bad behavior, or having been born into poverty, or to bad parents. For many of us from all backgrounds, it is unresolved trauma, often experienced at the hands of those who are supposed to take care of us. We are indeed punished for these things, and the penitentiary is where that punishment takes place. And since much of the behavior which originally sends us to prison is rooted in and driven by mental and emotional health issues (like trauma), we often get a lot worse when we are put into a pit of despair devoid of color, life, excitement, stimulation and connections to our family and friends. That means we are primed to reoffend once we are released, and when we do, we are punished by being sent back to prison. We couldn't build it better to support a permanent revolving door if we tried.

I am not referring to traditional notions of institutionalization, which generally leave out one important aspect of incarceration—the starting point. People who wind up in prison have experienced things in their lives which caused them to commit crimes or to make mistakes which were against the law. Of course, the institutional nature of the system is far from helpful when it comes to therapeutic needs, but that's because it's not designed to therapize. It is designed to punish. When we take people who are spinning out and resorting to crime, and instead of addressing their issues right away, we bottle them up and stuff them in a cage, it wouldn't matter how much institutionalization we added on top. The original problems are still there, only made worse by stewing side by side with others in the same situation. The institution doesn't make us into criminals; it just fails to help us stop being criminals. We seldom receive whatever it is we need to become invested in our communities, to build new identities outside of criminality, and to construct successful lives once we are released. Instead, we are left to simmer.

Unsurprisingly, the United States has produced high rates of recidivism for as long as we've kept track; those who are released from prison usually return in short order. The most recent data is in line with the historical trends: 82% of all released prisoners were rearrested within 10 years of their release from prison, and 61% of all released prisoners wound up back in prison.[227] We are punished for being punished, locked in a cage with other people who need help and support, then ignored until the clock runs out and we can be tossed back out onto the streets, usually untherapized and uneducated. I will offer solutions to this common approach to corrections in the final chapters of this book, after we have dealt with the trope of prison as a paradox. It's enough for now to point to the obvious futility of operating such a system, that is, unless the real goal is not rehabilitation at all. If the real goal were keeping prisons full and employees working, then the current system is humming away just fine, churning out a final product that appears to be perfectly in line with that goal.

Chapter 8

Prison as a Paradox

"In this age of mixing and hybridity, popular culture, particularly the world of movies, constitutes a new frontier providing a sense of movement, of pulling away from the familiar and journeying into and beyond the world of the other. This is especially true for those folks who really do not have much money or a lot of time as well as for the rest of us. Movies remain the perfect vehicle for the introduction of certain ritual rites of passage that come to stand for the quintessential experience of border crossing for everyone who wants to take a look at a difference and the different without having to experientially engage 'the other.'"[228] —bell hooks*

"prison culture—a society committed to the construction of prisons and the warehousing of mass numbers of people with little regard for the complexities of their lives, the lives of those hired to confine them, and the communities that surround them."[229]
—Michelle Brown*

The scene opens onto a massive prison yard with weightlifters in one corner, basketball players in another, and a large group of bleachers on the far side. The story's outlaw, Scofield, is using a quarter to work a screw out of a set of bleachers—all part of his master plan to break his brother out—but he's interrupted by someone who insists, "wrong piece of real estate, fish. It belongs to T-Bag."[230] As if summoned by the mention of his name, T-Bag appears out of nowhere. The camera locks on and zooms in. He has a striking hairline, a recognizable strut, and a set of pointy features that make him stand out from everyone else. But he's not alone. A group of white men flank him on either side, and directly next to him is a young, thin character who is meekly holding T-Bag's pocket, which has been pulled inside out. We know what this means, but not because anyone has explained it. It's just that, you know, prison is weird and creepy, so of course this guy can get away with forcing someone to perform acts of submission. It must be someone he is using for sex. Or maybe it's just a statement of domination. In any event, it doesn't make sense, but since it's prison, it kind of does. Prison is where we send people who commit crimes—for rehabilitation, for punishment, for containment—yet prison as a paradox is a place certain to increase criminality and *worsen* trauma.

Whenever prison is depicted as an evil puzzle full of unwritten rules and mysterious characters, prison as a paradox is on full display. Sometimes it's violent images, often cloaked in comedy, like the "don't drop the soap" line, which has shown up in prison films so often it's almost expected. The sexual assault cliché is so widely recognized that it's no longer shocking or taboo, as evidence by a 2002 commercial for 7-UP where a man passes cans of soda between jail cell bars until he drops one and says, "I'm not picking that up."[231] The "joke" is implicit: *you know, because he might be raped.* The ad ends with a more direct depiction of sexual assault as a man inside the prison embraces the spokesman without permission. As the camera pans out, presumably to abandon him inside, the victim pleads, "okay, that's enough being friends ...where are you guys going?!" As viewers, we don't know why picking up a can of soda would result in a sexual assault, nor why the crew would walk out on their coworker ignoring his pleas for help. But the prison setting allows us to plug in monsters in place of humans, and once we do that, raping someone just because they bend over seems a bit less nonsensical. These are prisoners we are talking about, after all. They are characters designed to make the spine tingle and the stomach turn. On second thought, maybe it all makes sense after all.

There is no shortage of paradoxical content slipped into prison films to aid in the creation of the eerie feeling prison media is supposed to evoke. For most of us, prison is an unfamiliar place which we have no interest in occupying, a situation which aids in our acceptance of otherwise bizarre behavior and baffling norms. In cinema, we learn that prison is candy bars on pillows when a new fish arrives, a sign that someone has already "claimed" that person as a sex slave and is making them property.[232] It's getting your parole approved by telling the parole board to go to hell, but only after decades of being denied for telling them you found religion or sought out self-improvement.[233] It's explanations that don't make sense, like going to prison "turns you gay," or institutionalization is guaranteed. It's in depictions of prison capitalism where bartering is done in odd ways and for odd things which appear worthless.[234] These depictions are not necessarily untrue, but they are necessarily out of context, added solely to enhance the spectacle value of the final product.

The end result of depictions of prison as a paradox is an understanding of prison as a confusing institution packed with vile monsters where unwritten rules place everyone in the role of either victim or perpetrator. However, this trope varies from the others in an important way. Instead of revealing the prison system as ultimately effective and necessary, the trope of prison as a paradox often works to expose the ineptness of the prison industrial complex, along with the massive toll, both economic and human, that it forces society to pay.

In 1967, *Cool Hand Luke* introduced viewers to one of cinema's favorite redeemed outlaws, a decorated war veteran who is sent to prison for destruction of public property. *The New York Times* called Luke a "victim not only of the brutality and sadistic discipline of his captors, but also . . . the indirect cruelty that comes from the idolization in the eyes of his fellow prisoners and, finally, of himself."[235] This somewhat confusing description of "cruelty that comes from idolization" is a great starting point for the trope of prison as a paradox, for seldom is idolization an act that can be described as cruel. Yet as Luke gains the respect of his new friends through his persistent over-the-top antics (in one scene he eats 50 eggs in a row to win a bet), he seems to become increasingly despondent at his inability to escape the confines of the prison. It doesn't matter how much Luke redeems himself; he is still stuck in jail. The admiration of his friends becomes a burden, and viewers are confronted with a confusing example of the prison environment: the trope of prison as a paradox. Unlike films set in maximum security prisons or on death row—places where punishment is no longer aimed at rehabilitating, but rather at threat containment and human disposal—films set in work camps or low level prisons, like *Cool Hand Luke,* frame abuse at the hands of guards as confusing and distasteful, not simply as penance for crimes committed.

Luke eventually escapes, cutting a hole through the cellblock's wooden floor and slipping away undetected during a celebration. But his freedom is short-lived, and upon his recapture, he is paraded before his peers, shackled with a set of ankle chains, and beaten by the warden, who quips, "what we've got here is failure to communicate. Some men you just can't reach . . . I don't like it any more than you." The warden's comments and the accompanying public spectacle of punishment paint prison as a place where people are not only physically abused, but where that abuse comes at the hands of a system that "doesn't like it any more than you," a paradox indeed. Confusing cruelty at the hands of prison employees is a sure sign that the trope of prison as a paradox is in full force. Unlike Wetmore's sadistic abuse of those on death row in *The Green Mile*, this lawman doesn't enjoy his duties, and *we* certainly don't want him to keep hitting Luke. In such scenes, our frustration as viewers winds up focused squarely on the prison system and those who operate it. *How is this supposed to rehabilitate anyone?*

Luke's nemesis in the film is Boss Godfrey, an obstinate lawman who always wears large, mirrored sunglasses to prevent anyone from seeing his eye.[236] He seemingly never speaks, and when a prisoner asks Luke one day, "Doesn't he ever talk?" Godfrey fittingly shoots a bird, to which Luke responds, "I think he just said something." Boss Godfrey sees, yet he is never seen, and he communicates without speaking, leaving viewers (and those he is watching) unsure of exactly what to think about this lawman.

In *Discipline and Punish: The Birth of the Prison*, Foucault describes the invention and utilization of an architectural device called the panopticon—an organizational prison system in which every individual can be supervised by a single overseer, while none of the observed can view their observer. "The major effect of the panopticon," contends Foucault, is "to induce in the inmate a state of conscious and permanent visibility that assures the automatic functioning of power."[237] It's so automatic that eventually those in the system tend to just give up and behave, disciplining themselves as if they are being observed even when they are not. Self-discipline is accomplished through the creation of a paradox where the observed cannot know when they are being watched, who is watching, or what the observation is directed at uncovering, yet they must always suspect that they are under surveillance. As such, they begin to surveil themselves.

Foucault's panoptic power, "visible and unverifiable," is

personified in the metonym of Boss Godfrey and his permanent sunglasses.[238] Godfrey is constantly visible, but his mirrored shades make it impossible for anyone to know where he is looking. In this Hollywood world of prison, the incarcerated can never truly know if they are being observed at any given moment even when the observer is visible. Godfrey could close his eyes and nobody would be the wiser. This sort of supervision provides the same sense of self-sustaining power that Foucault attributed to the physical structure of the penitentiary panopticon. The building is no longer necessary; the design works without it. Panopticons are paradoxical structures, whether they are physical spaces of deception or metaphoric power structures maintained by props like mirrored sunglasses. They work by whipping up a state of permanent, largely unfounded paranoia which can only be alleviated by regulating one's own behavior, conforming to whatever set of social norms is being enforced within that structure: religion, education, incarceration, or medicine. In Luke's case, the panopticon is aimed at keeping him in line with abusive prison policies, a goal that ultimately proves unsuccessful.

Cool Hand Luke dives into the trope of prison as a paradox as soon as Luke enters his cellblock for the first time, when a man who calls himself the floorwalker immediately begins reciting a long list of policies. Anyone who forgets his number, loses his spoon, fails to return his soda bottle, or is caught "playing grab ass" will be punished with a "night in the box." Despite the questions posed as he unemotionally recites the list, the floorwalker provides no additional insight as to what the rules mean, nor does he expound on what "the box" is. Later in the movie, "the box" is finally revealed as a plain, outhouse-sized building with no plumbing and bare floors. But Luke doesn't wind up there as punishment for breaking one of the recited rules. After learning his mother has recently passed away, Luke is pulled from his work detail and placed in the box because the warden believes he *might* plot an escape. Even the officer who locks the door appears disturbed by his duty, sheepishly offering, "Sorry Luke, I am just doing my job." Luke responds for the audience: "Calling it your job don't make it right, boss." Officers who are offended by their own official duties provide viewers with an image of prison as a paradox, a place so confusing and dangerous that even the officials don't understand or appreciate the rules.

Later, the trope of prison as a paradox is reiterated in perhaps the most torturous scene in the film, when Luke is returned to the prison after a second escape attempt and ordered to repeatedly dig a ditch then refill it as punishment. The task takes place in full view of the others in the camp, and it is meant to serve as an example of the prison's unquestionable and inescapable authority, usually used to force those inside to participate in pointless, debasing activities. The ditch-digging exercise also seems an effort to break the will of the stubborn outlaw, and it appears for a moment to have been successful, as even Luke claims, "they broke me." Or course, the pointless punishment is also a metonym for the frustration felt by millions of citizens ensnared in the contemporary punishment machine, where treatment and training are often ignored in favor of cheap labor and pointless job assignments. Prison as a paradox often opens such spaces of reconsideration, allowing (or forcing) audiences to note the complicity of the system in maintaining the status quo of packed prisons and sky-high recidivism.

That's the silver lining in representations of prison as a paradox. Unlike the tropes of prison as a playground and prison as penance, where our frustration is focused squarely on bad actors inside the prison, representation of prison as a paradox often emphasize the short-comings of the prison. When even the most extreme punitive sanctions at an officer's disposal are incapable of compelling rehabilitation, the system is exposed as fundamentally ineffective and poorly designed. It is at this point that producers often step in to allow prison as a playground to do the work the guards cannot, like happened in the final murder scene in *Short Eyes* and the rape scene in *American History X*.

Similar scenes depicting prison as a paradox appear in other prison films, whenever the outlaw is subjected to official treatment that leaves viewers confused or even indignant. In *The Green Mile,* representations of prison as penance give way to the archetype of prison as a paradox in the conclusion, when John Coffey, an innocent man who can heal the sick, is nonetheless executed for crimes he did not commit. Adding insult to injury, the victim's family is in the crowd, watching the execution with bitter enjoyment. Viewers have no control over whether Coffey will die, and it seems that neither does the film's lawman, Officer Edgecomb, who is convinced of Coffey's innocence. At a pivotal point in the movie, a distressed Edgecomb asks Coffey, "Tell me what you want me to do. Do you want me to take you out of here? Just let you run away? See how far you could get?" Edgecomb does not offer to file an appeal on behalf of Coffey, to contact the governor and request a pardon, or to seek any sort of legal remedy to the situation; he only asks Coffey if he wants him to "take him out of here," presumably to run from authorities for the rest of his life. In prison as a paradox, viewers often meet guards who recognize the fundamental ineffectiveness of the prison industrial complex when it comes to rehabilitation or righteous punishment. The system is the problem in prison as a paradox, and even those who operate it understand it's limitations and recognize its inability to accommodate true redemption.

Coffey's situation is a riddle with no solution, a paradox that ultimately leads to a pointless death. Edgecomb, a man intimately involved in the penal system, believes that the only possible solution to Coffey's imminent execution is to simply sneak the man out a back door when nobody is looking. This scene serves as a symbolic Javert suicide, as the obstinate lawman is unable to continue thoughtlessly performing his official duty. Instead, he decides to let the Dead Man Walking stroll out of prison, an act that will almost certainly land *him* in prison. His offer is quickly refused, however, in another paradoxical moment, when Coffey responds, "Why would you do such a foolish thing?" and accepts his own execution for a crime he did not commit. His calm demeanor moves the representation from prison as a paradox back to the more comfortable ground of prison as penance with a performance of a resigned Dead Man Walking.[239] As Yousman suggests, "such media images and narratives construct the penal system as just, as a flawed but ultimately functional institution."[240] In such an oxymoronic misguided-yet-functional institution, a few mistakes are acceptable if the punishment machine is to continue to operate on a massive level. Remember, Coffey is surrounded by other men who *are* guilty, and some of them are unrepentant all the way up to their deaths. So even though it's sad that this one innocent man had to die, what else can you expect society to do with the monsters dreamed up by Hollywood except to put them on death row. If we make a few mistakes, perhaps that's just the cost of justice. And anyway, the man who died didn't seem to mind so much.

In *Dead Man Walking,* the trope of prison as a paradox is demonstrated as the film's main character, Matthew, is prepared for execution. Throughout the film, despite his guilt, Matthew continues to insist that he is innocent, although his brand of innocence is not likely to win him much sympathy from the viewer, for, by his own admission, he stood by and watched a rape and double murder unfold without intervening. As the film develops,

Matthew is repeatedly portrayed as a cliché "bad guy"—racist, sexist, unrepentant, and downright mean. In one scene, he endorses Hitler and white supremacy, proclaiming the Holocaust has "never been proven." In another scene, he defends his hatred of black folks, calling them "lazy welfare-taking coloreds sucking up tax dollars." His reprehensible behavior is eventually derided by his religious advisor, who angrily explains, "You are making it so easy for them to kill you, coming across as some sort of a crazed-animal Nazi, racist mad dog who deserves to die." The fourth wall is all but broken; the line is for us, the viewer, as much as for Matthew, the film's outlaw. It's always easier to accept the death or pain of someone who we feel deserves it than to watch the innocent suffer, and the paradox is softened by suggesting that even when the system is wrong, it's still right. We might not want Matthew to die, but if the punishment machine must turn out a few errors, let this monster be one of them.

Everything changes just minutes before his execution, when Matthew confesses to committing the rape and murder (not just witnessing them), removing any remaining sense of apprehension viewers may have felt about putting an innocent man to death. As previously discussed, the last-minute confession also shifts the representation of prison as a paradox to prison as penance, leaving viewers with a cozy, final impression that, despite its confusing and extensive flaws, perhaps the system *can* be effective. After all, it finally got this bad guy to confess when nothing else could. Had the directors stuck with the theme of paradox until the end, we would have walked away scratching our heads and wondering, "should the prisons system be updated?" But lucky for viewers, they made it easy on us by updating the trope of prison as a paradox to a portrayal of prison as penance, allowing us to exit the theatre content in the illusion that our righteous system of punishment is functional despite its flaws.

In the trope of prison as a paradox, the penitentiary is depicted as a self-perpetuating system of ineffective discipline which reinforces the very antisocial behavior it is intended to correct. In *Life*, the trope of prison as a paradox is exemplified in the cornbread diatribe, in which Rayford Gibson responds to a larger man's demand for his cornbread with threats of "consequences and repercussions." The resulting one-sided fistfight is almost identical to a scene in *Cool Hand Luke*, and both fights present the trope of prison as a paradox—they simply don't make sense. Gibson and Luke both instigate a fight with the largest man in the prison, both continue to fight well past the point of defeat, and both fights take place in plain view of guards who fail to intervene. After the fights, both men are awarded a strange sort of respect from the rest of the prison, as if the fact that someone would needlessly subject themselves to a brutal beating while trying to hurt someone else is worthy of some sort of bizarre adoration (patriarchal nonsense aside). None of it adds up, but we play along anyway because the story is set in prison, and after all, that place is confusing and terrible. In the trope of prison as a paradox, prison is a place where idolization is cruel and self-destruction is respectable, where being beaten is prideworthy and the guards watch the fights, where dropping the soap gets you raped, and where giving up on redemption is often the only way to achieve it. Prison as a paradox is a place where innocent people go to die, and where even the guards recognize the injustice designed into the system. Unlike the other films mentioned in this chapter, at the end of *Life*, producers stuck with the paradox trope, allowing viewers to not only walk away discontent with the prison system depicted, but also allowing us to celebrate the successful escape of our outlaws, who we come to understand could not have achieved their redemption any other way. The system might be ineffective, but at least these outlaws managed to break out.

A correctional system that endorses or encourages violent behavior between those it claims to rehabilitate is incapable of effecting rehabilitation. A hyper-sexualized, violent environment is not the sort of place one heads to for self-improvement. Confusing rules and abusive neighbors are not what most of us want in our communities. Yet unlike prison as a playground or prison as penance, there is a space opened up in representations of prison as a paradox wherein our indignation, which would otherwise be directed toward the depraved actions of those in prison, is instead directed toward the prison system, which is shown to be the cause of many of the problems it claims to fix. In sum, where the trope of prison as a playground perpetuates stereotypes of those in prison as hedonistic monsters, and the trope of prison as penance reinforces the idea that the penitentiary is the only way to protect society from those unrepentant monsters, the trope of prison as a paradox frequently emphasizes the prison's culpability in creating and sustaining the very behavior it claims to be punishing, painting the prison industrial complex as a mismanaged and misguided institution of suffering that does more damage than good. Paradoxical prisons don't redeem outlaws.

The inefficacy and confusion built into the prison industrial complex is always the central theme in representations of prison as a paradox. When extreme methods of official punishment that border on torture are nonetheless shown to be unproductive, as is frequently the case in representations of prison as a paradox, the viewer is forced to question the effectiveness of the entire punishment machine. While the tropes of prison as a playground and prison as penance always endorse the necessity of an eternally-expanding prison industrial complex, the trope of prison as a paradox can be deployed to expose the penitentiary as a brutal-yet-ineffective machine of punishment that does more harm than good. Unfortunately, we also get a predictably foul dose of monsters who are beyond redemption in most paradox narratives, and even though we might not mind "Cool Hand" Luke or Andy Dufresne living next door to us, we probably don't want the rest of the characters we know from prison films to move in across the street.

Prison is a paradox. It's designed to be confusing. I almost received a disciplinary ticket my first day in the joint, but not because I was misbehaving. I left my cell door open when I wasn't sure if I should shut it after chow. Those in charge expected everyone arriving to understand the rules before we arrived. Of course, there are plenty of riddles to be solved, but they are usually in the form of official policy and unwritten rules concerning those in positions of power. There is a so-called "convict code" that guides interactions amongst those inside, but it is not a creepy list of institutionalized behavior or a guide to victimizing others.[241] It's the same list of unofficial rules that you would want implemented if you were forced into a confined space with hundreds of strangers: mutual respect, mind your own business, never back down, don't get too close to those in power, and don't snitch. It's not a list of rules about who to abuse or regulation regarding pocket-holding on the yard. Beyond the paradox of policy lies the reality of flesh and blood. The official rules are what usually get us in trouble, not the people with whom we share a cell.

The entire system is a paradox, and it doesn't take long to notice from the inside. A few days after I arrived in prison, I became aware of a teenager a few cells down who was struggling with the grit of forced isolation. He asked for psychiatric help every time a guard walked past, but each told him the same thing—they would get to him whenever the doctor had time. The kid found himself in quite a bind, but not one which he felt was beyond solution. After a few days of being put off, he slammed his hand in the cell door after chow one morning, and what do you know—they took him down to medical right away, then directly to a psychiatric appointment.

He wasn't the only one. Every day I saw people who were struggling with physical disabilities, emotional turmoil, trauma, learning disorders, and psychiatric conditions, and we were all in the same situation—left to fend for ourselves and navigate a system designed to confuse and disorient us at every turn. The best they could hope for was a daily visit to the medication line and a weekly check-in with their case worker. The paradox is how anyone could expect such a system to result in anything except worsening symptoms.

The policy is the paradox. Those who are navigating those policies must be clever to survive. Movie producers who lean into the trope of prison as a paradox should be aware of the methods they use and the stereotypes they deploy if they wish to avoid targeting those in prison rather than the prison itself. There are ways to make cinema that is titillating and engaging without turning those of us who have been to prison into monsters behind bars.

Chapter 9

Privileging Perspectives from Inside the "Belly of the Beast"[242]

"A cacophony of anguish, five-stories high, thirty cells long, packed with flesh. The prison has more than five-thousand steel-barred cells—tear-stained concrete boxes filled with ink-stained concrete men.[243] *It spreads out for 52 acres enclosed by a 34-foot-high wall, every inch of it covered in razor wire, bird nests, and the rotting carcasses of animals that became ensnared in the web of blades. This is Jackson State Prison, or the Michigan State Prison, or the Charles Egeler Reception and Guidance Center—the name changes periodically to keep the critics on their heels. I am inmate 470236.*[244] *–Benjamin Boyce*

"It is not that what is necessary to open up space of critique is a better assessment of the real, some carful replica of contemporary prison conditions, but rather penal conventions and narrative structures which challenge the penal spectator to interrogate punishment, to leave them with uneasy contradictions and uncertain absences in resolution—and their place in that problematic."[245]
—Michelle Brown

Thus far this book has explored contemporary television and film representations of the prison industrial complex, focusing on the schism between de Certeau's condensed and edited "referential reality" created with information gleamed from film, and the actual environment of prison, which most viewers will never experience firsthand. The archetypal characters of the outlaw seeking redemption and the lawman who refuses to give it to him have been shown to reappear time and again in cinematic representations of prison. The previous chapters explored various ways such cinematic portrayals work to reinforce the viewer's belief in the necessity of a permanently expanding, ever-harsher prison industrial complex. When the stories we use to explain the world come solely from Hollywood, we tend to view penitentiaries as a vital prerequisite for our continued safety.

Cinematic representations of prison have become thorns in the sides of authors and academics seeking to educate the public as to the shortcomings of the prison industrial complex, as we must consistently compete with a barrage of media stereotypes. To overcome this barrier, an increasing number of individuals have taken up the pen from a position inside prison walls, and as Nellis posits:

> "The newly emergent 'convict criminology,' produced in the USA by ex-cons (usually imprisoned as a result of the 'war on drugs') who have subsequently become academics, arguably enables criminology in general to go beyond the best of what it has said hitherto about release and resettlement.[246]

I am one of these academics who came from inside those walls. The largest walled prison on Earth is still in operation in Jackson, Michigan, although the official title disappeared when they broke the administrative duties of the prison into different sections overseen by different officials.[247] My incarceration stemmed from an addiction in a country that has the gall to call itself the land of the free while incarcerating people who use drugs, a policy that works to drive the price of those drugs up by 10,000% (or more).[248] Although academics will frequently find themselves at a disadvantage when competing against Hollywood's never-ending spectacle of punishment, the voices of we who have seen the system from the inside are invaluable for supplementing the glamorous media tropes of playground, penance, and paradox with more concrete representations of the prison experience as a whole.

In addition to firsthand narratives penned from within prison, the last decade has seen the emergence and expansion of a number of activist organizations devoted to the project of media-literacy education, a form of critical reasoning aimed at challenging problematic representations. Media literacy education provides consumers with the tools necessary to question distorted images on television and in movies, and to actively undo our collective miseducation concerning the horrors and infectiveness of mass incarceration.[249] In the following pages, I will outline the efforts of some of the authors, academics, artists and activists who are already working both inside and outside of prison to reveal the truth about what goes on behind penitentiary walls. I end with a firsthand account of my time in prison as a victim of the war on drugs, and a description of the journey into academia which it inspired.

From Banal to Bizarre

Mumia Abu-Jamal is an activist, journalist and radio personality who was sentenced to death for the murder of a police officer in 1982.[250] He has been incarcerated in a maximum-security Pennsylvania prison ever since his conviction, and for a long time he was locked up on death row, until, following a long legal battle, his death sentence was commuted to life in 2011.[251] Abu-Jamal, who *The New York Times* has referred to as "perhaps the world's best known death row inmate," has written a number of books detailing his life behind bars.[252] In an excerpt from one of his most popular texts, *Live From Death Row,* Abu-Jamal describes how "Life here oscillates between the banal and the bizarre."[253] This is not a description of the dark and threatening atmosphere of Shawshank Prison or of *The Green Mile's* death row. There is no suggestion of the self-produced entertainment seen in *Cool Hand Luke's* antics or *Prison Break's* tattoo mysteries, nor the cushion of comedy, which makes such depictions easier to stomach. This is a world of endless wasted time infrequently interrupted by the odd behavior of those who are struggling to survive what often borders on psychological torture.

Abu-Jamal pinpoints the break between the prison he lives in and those typically portrayed in film. In the cinematic representation, the viewer has no patience for the banal, and so there is no oscillation. Producers stick to the bizarre. But as Abu-Jamal emphasizes throughout the text, the banal is the dominating theme in his prison experience, and the bizarre is an infrequent break from "The mind-numbing, soul-killing savage sameness that makes each day an echo of the day before, with neither thought nor hope of growth," making "prison the abode of spirit death."[254] There is no playground for Abu-Jamal to manipulate, no penance that can be served on his way to redemption, and no way to escape the paradox of prolonged suffering he describes. The real prison industrial complex that Abu-Jamal lives within is a blunt tool of punishment which acts with brutal consistency upon each of its residents. It's hard to walk away from such descriptions without feeling as if prisons are doing active damage to those within them. And it's not just those behind the bars who are affected by the reality of incarceration.

Other authors have explored the prison system from the position of correctional officers. In one such book, *New Jack: Guarding Sing Sing,* which *The Denver Post* called "experimental journalism at its best," author Ted Conover details his experiences as a

Corrections Officer in New York's most infamous state prison.[255] Conover wasn't your normal correctional officer. He only took the job because he wanted to write a story about the prison, but they wouldn't allow him inside: the training facility for guards and the prison itself were "off limits to journalists—no exceptions, end of conversation."[256] So he decided to become a guard.

As an officer, Conover's perspective is different from Abu-Jamal's: "it was a life sentence in eight-hour shifts."[257] But he echoes similar themes of anguish and hopelessness as defining characteristics of his prison experience:

> "You feel it along the walls inside, hard like a blow
> to the head; see it on the walls outside, thick,
> blank, and doorless; smell it in the air that assaults
> your face in certain tunnels, a stale and acrid taste
> of male anger, resentment, and boredom . . . walls
> built not to shelter but to constrain."[258]

Conover's "life sentence" is described throughout the book as an emotionally exhausting role wherein he and his fellow officers "adopted blank, tough expressions that betrayed no weakness or curiosity, no disgust or delight . . . Was this only about closing the blinds on your own soul so they couldn't see in?"[259] On Christmas Day, Conover describes the unspoken obligation to "deny it. Christmas spirit—generosity, forgiveness, goodwill toward men—ran pretty much counter to what we were supposed to be doing. Prison was for punishment; it wasn't ours to forgive."[260] On New Year's Eve, a night when most people celebrate new beginnings, Conover explains, "unlike my friends, they [incarcerated people] weren't celebrating the arrival of the New Year so much, it seemed, as closing the book on the old."[261] Seldom does anyone who has actually spent time in prison (guard or guarded) describe the experience as redemptive, disciplinary or rehabilitative. These themes are always drowned out by the chorus of anguish which pours forth from our pens when we sit down to describe what we have seen. The prison industrial complex is currently a machine of pointless torture. And yet, despite existing within a system designed to kill the spirit and deaden the mind, much beauty pours forth from those institutional spaces, revealing a well of untapped potential.

Captured Words/Free Thoughts

In winter 2022, I met up with a small group of activists in an office space on the downtown Denver campus of Colorado University. We were there to celebrate the publication of the 18th edition of *Captured Words/Free Thoughts,* an annual magazine packed with art, poetry and prose inspired inside prison walls. We were also there to package and mail out almost four hundred copies of the magazine to incarcerated artists and their family members. The pieces published always tell a story, and in 2022, two main themes rose to the surface: the social awakening surrounding Black Lives Matter, and COVID-19 protocols in prison. Both events had inspired incredibly vivid art, and now it was time to share it with the world. The voices contained in this magazine and others like it are not hyperviolent or menacing. They are teachers and students, philosophers and crafters. Their work often can't be contained on the page.

And so that project has expanded to the "new digital commons," the land of podcasting.[262] Every year I ask my on-campus students to volunteer their time and their voices to record some of the poems sent in by incarcerated people, to give voice back to the silenced. The productions are powerful and public, but they lack the shiny gloss of Hollywood rape scenes and prison yard fights. They are narratives of people dealing with the stuff that people deal with in prison: boredom, depression, hopelessness, confusion, and disheartening loss of identity. But they are also voices of self-improvement and dedication, of overcoming odds and breaking stereotypes. The finalized episodes are available free of charge on *The Dr. Junkie Show*.[263]

I am not the first ex-incarcerated person to pick up the microphone and step into the world of podcasting. The award-winning prison-based podcast *Ear Hustle* has released ten seasons of episodes, along with an accompanying book. The hosts represent both sides of prison walls. Nigel Woods is an activist who works with incarcerated people, and Earlonne Woods is one of the show's hosts who was locked up in San Quentin Prison for the first two seasons before his release. Other hosts are still working from inside prison, focusing on art, stories, beliefs, poetry, music, and education.

The stories shared by authors in *Captured Words/Free Thoughts* and by the hosts of *Ear Hustle* are seldom tales of violence, sexual assault or monsters lurking in the dark. Those things sometimes show up because prison is a place where we throw people who need help, and humans often do some awful things when put in awful situations. But these productions seek to update our public narrative about crime and punishment. The redemption we only get to see a very few characters achieve in prison cinema is on full display in every episode of *Ear Hustle*. Listeners walk away feeling like they might want to go to prison themselves, not to serve time, but to volunteer. In productions such as these, prison comes across as a place full of people who made some bad choices when put in bad situations, because that's what prison is. Most importantly, when you consume these media productions, it starts to feel like the US is doing something very wrong with our correctional system.

Judith Tannenbaum is the author of *Disguised as a Poem: My Years Teaching Poetry at San Quentin,* a book where she consistently notes the sense of despair and hopelessness that seems to predominate the prison environment and bleed into those of us who teach or volunteer our time inside.[264] At one point, Tannenbaum reveals her frustration at the rigidity of the system, envisioning "an image of prison as a brick wall I kept hurling my body against. I knew my body would certainly be crushed long before even the slightest of dents appeared in the brick wall."[265] In another section, she talks about one of her most outspoken students, and how she wonders if he "ever worried that prison might eventually wear down his capacity to be a human being out in the world."[266] Yet at the same time as she voices concerns that her students may be impacted by the inflexible prison system, she consistently humanizes those she speaks of, at one point explaining that, "the longing to be emotionally close to another creature [is] part of the human experience. A man or a woman in prison doesn't stop being human, and so, doesn't stop desiring closeness."[267] Tannenbaum's story lacks all of the spectacle and horror of traditional Hollywood productions, but it is packed with as much heartbreak and grit as any prison film. Such productions leave us with the impression that prison is an ineffective, inefficient machine of containment which does more damage than good. More importantly, we don't meet inmates, prisoners or offenders in the work of these activists; we meet people—artists, authors, parents and siblings.

When the damage done by the prison industrial complex is inflicted upon innocent youngsters, we ought to find ourselves particularly indignant. An early victim of what would later be termed "The Satanic Panic," Damien Echols served nearly two decades on Arkansas's death row after being convicted of three murders when he was just eighteen years old.[268] His sentence was eventually commuted to "time-served" in 2012, after much public attention and three separate HBO documentaries concerning the case led prosecutors to reexamine some questionable evidence. Shortly after his release from prison, Echols published *Life After Death,* a gritty memoir detailing his time behind bars. In the text, Echols notes the ability of the prison industrial complex to produce something akin to the opposite of rehabilitation, to "send a man to prison for writing bad checks and then torment him there until he becomes a violent offender."[269] He goes on to explain life inside:

> "On an average day there is nothing kind, gener-
> ous, caring, or sensitive within these walls. The
> energy directed at you is hatred, rage, disgust,
> stupidity, ignorance, and brutality. It affects you
> in mind, body, and soul, much like a physical
> beating. The pressure is relentless and unending.
> Soon you walk with your shoulders slumped and
> your head down, like a beast that's used to being
> kicked."[270]

In Echol's world, there was no sensational journey to interrupt the banality of "this hell devoid of anything that makes life worth-while."[271] The spectacle of punishment gives way to the comradery of flesh and blood, and readers can't help but feel like something isn't quite right with our punishment machine.

Our understanding of incarceration is updated when authors focus on the paradoxical qualities of the penitentiary, detailing a torturous design which virtually ensures everyone who winds up there will be traumatized before they leave.[272] Stephen Hartnett poetically details his experiences teaching creative writing classes to incarcerated students:

> *reeling from the stifling ugliness*
> *of gray walls gray clothing gray*
> *food gray soul gray dismal*
> *gray no bright colors*
> *no music no laughter no beauty.*[273]

Incarcerated author Amos Rogers similarly described the dehumanization of life behind bars, stating, "prison is being told what you can wear, what you can own, what you can eat, how much sun and fresh air you can enjoy, and when you can call home, if you have a home."[274] Their stories speak volumes to the plight of the those locked up for extended periods inside these stressful environments. When the tropes of prison as a playground, prison as penance, and prison as a paradox give way to firsthand accounts from inside the system, the prison industrial complex is exposed as the massive, ineffective dungeon it has become.

Media Literacy Education

In addition to emphasizing perspectives offered in firsthand prison narratives, many have endorsed the idea of expanded media-literacy education campaigns designed to help consumers understand what they are learning from media.[275] The recipe for advertisement is always the same: create or pinpoint a consumer need, then offer a solution. The cinematic tropes of prison create a problem through irredeemably evil characters who cause viewers to feel as if we can never truly be safe, then they offer a solution in the form of an expensive product, the prison industrial complex. We can learn to resist both messages, but not unless we understand what is being communicated and actively seek out personal information to offset the drama offered by our screens. In addition to firsthand narratives from within the prison industrial complex, numerous organizations devoted to media-literacy education are utilizing contemporary forms of media to share information, attempting to reveal a more nuanced picture of prison than what is typically offered in Hollywood representations. Along with narratives challenging the status quo of mass incarceration, new and specialized sources for news media are also opening spaces for rethinking stereotypes and norms of incarceration.

Founded in 1970, *Free Press* is a well-established activism group devoted to encouraging transparency by exposing the elaborate connections between multinational corporations and mainstream media. *Free Press* looks to combat what it calls "corporate control over our print media" through ensuring "that the public has a seat at the table."[276] Their website is flashy and interactive, and their stories focus on social justice issues and systemic problems related to power and oppression. Similarly, *The Marshall Project* publishes work focused on the ineptness of the prison system and the scarring nature of its various techniques of domination, and most of their authors are current or formers residents of prison. *Filter Magazine* is a press organization devoted to harm reduction and ending the war on drugs, and their articles typically aim to expose the faulty design of our current drug policies, which ensure the problem will continue to get worse until we update the system. Organizations such as these offer resources to supplement the limited and biased perspective supplied by Hollywood prison cinema, providing movie-happy consumers with legitimate information to enrich our junk food media diets. They serve as valuable hubs for social justice activists in search of support, resources, or content.

In addition to media-literacy education, the documentary film presents a particularly effective tool for combatting the misinformation offered by prison cinema, for despite its lack of a full pre-written script, it uses the same tools of visual and audio representation that draw viewers to fictional prison films. Although this film genre is as vulnerable to edits, cuts, and context manipulation as any other, it nonetheless presents an alternative to the purely fictional prison narrative, and as such, it serves to richen viewer knowledge of hidden spaces, including the prison industrial complex. Plus, it serves as competition for the Hollywood spectacle;

it pushes the same buttons, so to speak, by playing with the same senses (sight and sound) as any other film. As Marshall McLuhan reminds us, "the medium is the message."[277] People looking for films to consume may not find other forms of media satisfactory to scratch that itch. They may, however, find themselves content with documentary evidence.

This brief list of alternative media resources is only the tip of the iceberg when it comes to the numerous organizations working to reform society's notion of mainstream media. There are more people doing this work every year. In addition to television and the big screen, podcasting and social media are opening avenues of knowledge and providing access to an audience easier than ever before. These alternatives to spectacle all allow for an amplification of voices that might otherwise be inaudible amongst the cacophony of media noise we are bombarded with daily. But they are no match for the flood of superhero films and scandal stories Hollywood throws at us each year. To really push back against the inundation of movie messages, we must establish and sustain a media landscape that counters the problematic messages we are force-fed daily. We must create a new form of responsible media—an updated spectacle.

The movies and television shows discussed throughout this book have repeatedly confirmed the existence of three representational tropes: prison as a playground, prison as penance, and prison as a paradox. These stereotypical prison representations provide viewers with information concerning a typical prison environment, and without any firsthand knowledge to authenticate or to disprove what is seen, the movie or television representation becomes conflated with reality in our minds. It doesn't take long for the knowledge learned from prison films to lead to tacit approval of the prison industrial complex, and by proxy, of its continued growth and harshening. As Abu-Jamal laments, "prisons have become a warped rite of passage, a malevolent mark of manhood, and a dark expectation."[278] Yet, as Conover counters, "can *rite of passage* possibly be the correct term for a kind of suspended animation that leaves you older, weaker, less sexually attractive, and less connected to the community than before you went in?"[279]

A change is in the air, one that will challenge the current system's strict and unquestionable punitive grasp. The "convict criminologists" who authored the afore mentioned books, and those who will author the next generation, represent the foundational counterpart to Hollywood's glamorized prison environment. In addition, activist organizations dedicated to providing media-literacy education through online blogs and multimedia resources will continue to play a valuable role in disseminating information about prison conditions and operations, working to expose the intrinsic design issues of the prison industrial complex.

It may seem at first like these two things are disconnected: *what do books written by prisoners have to do with movies made in Hollywood?* But organizations like *The Marshall Project* are showing us that they aren't so far apart as we might think. Recent articles published in the "Life Inside" series, part of *The Marshall Project,* have titles like, "I Thought Going to Jail would get me Clean: I was Dead Wrong," and "I Did 340 Push-Ups a Day to Prepare for the TV Version of Prison: Then I got There," tempting readers to dive into articles that are, in many ways, alternatives to Hollywood's spectacle of punishment. But there is one important difference between mainstream media and stories published by *The Marshall Project*, and it comes down to where we wind up pointing the finger in the end of our journey. In many of the films described throughout this book, viewers either wind up blaming those in prison for their ongoing bad behavior, or we wind up unsure of where the blame belongs, and as such, unsure what exactly needs to change. But stories like those in *The Marshall Project* focus our blame squarely on the system, and more importantly, they usually provide clear targets for transformation. We can get out of the problematic stereotype business without shutting down the entire Hollywood machine of drama and spectacle. It just takes some deliberate effort.

We are a small step from the next era of media-literacy education, when we will stop cleaning up the mess *after* Hollywood makes it and instead try to prevent them from making it in the first place. To do that, we must compete. We need stories that play on the same human emotions as those we currently enjoy: love, hate, disgust, pain, loss, longing and lust. We need plots that force viewers to acknowledge systemic problems and point to the changes that need to happen. But we also need to keep viewers tuned in. It isn't as big of an update in the standards of production as we might have thought. It's just a matter of avoiding the easy path producers often take—the low hanging fruit where evil villains draw our ire by torturing the good guys. We have to figure out clever ways to include the system's complicity in the suffering of those in our films, and we ought to go the extra mile to weave in some sort of solution, a change that can be made to address the problems depicted. The spine tingling and cringe inducing scenes don't have to go away; they just need different characters and different endings.

Prison Education

Let's be real: prison is boring. There is nothing to do. Your friends and family are far away. The food is terrible and insufficient. You don't have many comfort items. That's kind of the point, at least in our current system. Our justice system assumes that humans are logical beings who all begin life on the same page, and who all make decisions from a universal set of values and morals. Then it labels anyone who breaks an arbitrary rule a "criminal" and places them in time-out, fully uninterested in why they acted differently than those around them. Of course, the new correctional system which myself and other activists propose will be different.[280] Whatever small amount of time people may need to be removed from their social circles will no longer be wasted on punishing them with banality and solitude. In practice, our hope is that removing people at all will become less common as we get better at our updated goal of preventing (not just punishing) crime. People who are convicted of crimes need tools for success, not lashes for failure. Prison should be a place stereotyped as an educational warehouse, an institution of perpetual betterment where everyone leaves with more certification than when they arrived. *You can't get out of that place without receiving training for something.*

This isn't pie in the sky dreaming. In fact, it's already happening in some areas of the country. Twice a week I lead college classes in two Colorado State Prisons. As every prison educator I have met will tell you, incarcerated students are, as a rule, the most dedicated and involved students we teach. More importantly, they seem to be in the best position of any students we have to use the content to its full potential, because they are receiving it with a long journey ahead of them, whereas many of those taking on-campus classes are already nearing their journey's predictable end—a degree followed by a steady career. More than most groups, incarcerated students need to learn how to communicate, how to deal with disagreements, how to overcome challenges, and how to manage difficult situations where their identities are contested. They are the people who should be offered the *most* education in any society, not the least. Their path to success is longer and more arduous than the average citizen. Their failures fall on the pocketbooks of taxpayers one way or another. It pays to prevent recidivism by giving them tools for success prior to their release.

In his celebratory piece describing prison education, "Communication, Social Justice and Joyful Commitment," Stephen Hartnett describes the value of teaching Communication classes to students who are locked up. His experiences mirror mine, for our students both explain to us over and over how they wish they had learned this content before they got in trouble, that:

> ". . . if they had only known how to communicate more effectively, they might have talked or written their way out of danger. Somewhere, somehow, whether it was in the kitchen or the principal's office, on the street or in the courtroom, dealing with a boss or a family member or a detective, greater communicative fluency could have made a life-changing difference. And so my students come to our classes and workshops looking for pragmatic answers: They expect me to bring to them the tools of persuasion, argumentation, better writing, and clearer thinking—not just because they want to land jobs on the outside but because they want redemption, they want to reclaim their lives from the numbness and mumbling bequeathed to them by years of neglect and violence."[281]

It's not just our opinions. The RAND corporation found that those who take college classes while in prison are 43% less likely to recidivate than those who do not.[282] They are also more likely to find and maintain stable employment after release.[283] That's largely because of the identity that comes with education, along with the tools we learn to utilize as strategies for life success. Walking out of prison with a college degree means walking out of prison with a stable, respectable identity outside that of "outlaw," a valuable tool for dealing with the Scarlet Letter of background checks which is sure to follow us for the rest of our lives. Michelle Alexander's New Jim Crow—the stigma of felony conviction—is directly contested by the stereotypes which accompany education and certification.[284] We fear and even hate criminals; we value and trust those whose education leads to certification (or degrees). Prison education changes prison stereotypes from the inside-out.

As I write this, my students just wrapped up a class called "Communication, Citizenship and Social Justice," and two incredible things happened as our time together neared its end. First, the students began to weave together content from weeks two and four, linked into week eight with a shout-out to the theory offered in week twelve. This happens in any successful class where writing is required, but it's always an incredible feeling as a teacher to recognize the various ways different students synthesize the same content to apply it to their unique perspectives in life. But this time somehow felt different than the normal on-campus course.

Together we had navigated a class about racism and white supremacy in the United States, a class where we followed Martin Luther King Jr.'s "moral arc" only to realize it is neither consistent nor guaranteed to proceed. We learned that women were left out of the Constitution deliberately because they weren't supposed to exist in political life, that the institution of white supremacy didn't go anywhere after the Civil War, that Lincoln didn't want to free the slaves outright, and that group after group has been forced to fight tooth and nail for basic human rights against self-described good people who thought they were doing the right thing.[285] We read about how, despite such bitter disagreements and contentious debates, this country has carried on for more than two hundred

135

years, working it out through our differences. The students loved it. Sure, it was challenging at times, and of course there was some pushback, just like there always is in classes that cover contentious topics. But these scholars worked through the content as well as any others, better in many ways. This despite the fact that Hollywood would have you believe that those in prison are usually unrepentant monsters who thrive on the continued victimization of others. That's never been my experience in prison, neither when I spent time there, nor as a teacher.

The people I have met in prison tend to be the opposite of Hollywood's bad guy. They are engaged and clever, and they can spot a connection a mile away. That's often what lands them—us—in prison in the first place. We who wind up with criminal records often lack the tools to thrive in this world via legitimate means, so when we spot an advantage which we appear to have over others around us—physical strength, willingness to engage in violence, lock picking, lying, theft, drug dealing, hustling, or any other antisocial trick—we take it. And just like anyone else, we begin to build an identity around those things that work, appreciating the way those aspects of our persona allow us to feel unique and powerful. Of course, when we are running the streets all day, we don't receive the education necessary to discover or develop alternative tools for success. When we settle for putting our smarts to use robbing banks, running scams, hustling people or stealing property, we are too busy to pursue the things that might otherwise come to define us—things like education and career aspirations. College programs in prison provide students with the tools to change them from incarcerated people into tax-paying citizens. It's fiscally, ethically and logically superior to the way we currently do things. And most importantly, it works to reduce recidivism.

That's the story that should be on the tip of anyone's tongue when it comes to prison and those who are trapped there. One way to force the hand of movie producers is to turn the prisons of our imaginations into a sort of magnet school for people who commit crimes. Prisons should be packed with therapists and medical professionals, drug treatment providers and counselors, college programs and GEDs, art teachers and philosophers, training certificates and PhDs. And as that happens, movie producers might actually have an original prison story on their hands, the first one in a long time. We can still lower the lights and turn on the creepy music. We can still pedal in spectacle and excitement. If the consumer demands these things, producers will continue to offer them regardless. But we can also reshape the stories which contain these dramatic events and rid them of the stereotypes and tropes which have been inseparable from them for more than a hundred years. The spectacle of punishment can be updated into a spectacle of education and rehabilitation.

> "What social interest is served by prisoners who remain illiterate? What social benefit is there in ignorance? How are people corrected while imprisoned if their education is outlawed? Who profits (other than the prison establishment itself) from stupid prisoners?"[286] —Mumia Abu-Jamal

Chapter 10

Then There's Me

"If we had the political will, we could use our resources and creativity to address the social issues that lead to crime—but we continue to use cages instead."[287] —Lori Pompa

"The earth is but one great ball. The borders, the barriers, the cages, the cells, the prisons of our lives, all originate in the false imagination of the minds of men."[288] —Mumia Abu-Jamal

"Most people who study crime and criminals study from the outside peering in, but I study on the inside peeping out—through prison bars."[289]—Kate Richards O'Hare

"Lights out!"

But the boys weren't ready for bed yet. Not tonight. It was Thanksgiving, and an odd energy had been building all day.

It started somewhere in the middle, although the cellblock was so massive it was hard to say for sure. Echoes made everything difficult to locate. But it seemed to sort of spread outward from the center, like each cell was catching the beat then tossing it on to the next.

> Oh Happy Day
> *oh happy day*
> Oh Happy Day
> *oh happy day*
> When Jesus washed
> *when Jesus washed...*

It was only one guy at first, then two, then four. But within a few lines, dozens of echoes were bouncing out of cells to join the chorus. I stood up and walked to the front of my cell to get a better look. A wall of bodies greeted me. It was the same wall of bodies that always greeted me, floor-to-ceiling, front, back and on both sides of the cellblock. The cacophonous jumble of grunts and shouted questions which normally overwhelmed my senses was suddenly a single chorus, ringing in unison. Everything else disappeared.

My sins away
My sins away
Oh Happy day
Oh happy day

As quickly as it started, it ended. The director of the flash mob attempted to lead his choir through another verse, but it wasn't possible. The chaos that had disappeared when the song began seemed immediately back to full volume, like it had never stopped. It was laughter and passionate conversation, always shouted loud enough to make it through the wall or ceiling, even if it was only meant for the person next door.

That noise is tattooed on my eardrums. It is baked into my neural map. It never turned all the way off, and I've been out for almost twenty years now. It was life and harmony, separate entities that, unordered, could simultaneously come together to produce something beautiful, then go back to their own solitary journeys. Such are the memories I have of prison and those inside. But stories such as these seldom make their way into Hollywood blockbusters unless they are spectacular enough to draw the attention of a crowd. A group of incarcerated people singing a religious song is nice, but a group of monsters murdering one another, now *that's* entertainment.

It turns out that I am not immune to the spectacle. When I discovered I was headed to prison, I started working out and eating everything I could get my hands on, desperately trying to gain weight and muscle to minimize the assaults I was sure would happen the second I got to the joint. I had been on the planet for twenty years, and throughout my life I had been taught that prison was a place where rowdy men scream "Fresh Fish!" at new arrivals, where rape and violence are par for the course, where everyone is either a victimizer or a victim, and damn if I was going to head into *that* place unprepared. If I was going to live where monsters live, I had better become a monster.

A deck of playing cards minus the jokers contains 52 individual cards. If you count aces as one, all the face cards as ten, and everything else at face value, they total 340. My plan was simple; I'd flip cards and do pushups, then flip more cards and do more pushups. Since I was in jail awaiting transfer to state prison, I had plenty of time. In a day I would go through the deck 2-3 times, more when my arms didn't give out. And in the meantime, I'd do sit-ups on the floor, pullups on the top bunk, and squats holding as many books as possible out in front of me. By the time I got to prison, I hardly recognized myself. I'd gained 15 pounds and my hair had grown out, but I was ready for war.

And then . . . war never came. Don't get me wrong, there was a lot of drama to get caught up in, and there were occasional fights. But that happens no matter who you lock in a confined area with limited resources. Tempers flare, and when you can't walk away, those tempers sometimes boil over. But I never experienced an incarcerated person attacking me or trying to sexually assault me. On the contrary, I had quite a few people take care of me while my money was in transport (it often doesn't arrive until days after we do). It seemed that my pushups had done little to prepare me for what I found in prison. I would have been better suited reading some communication books before I arrived.

The other incarcerated people were seldom a problem. But the bureaucracy of the penitentiary, that was another story. Prison is indeed set up to physically and emotionally torture us, but not at the hands of our fellow incarcerated people. The abuse comes from the system. And it is created by design. The system agreed to feed me every day while I was locked up, then it left me hungry. The system agreed to provide medical and mental health services, then it paroled me without any form of addiction treatment or post-incarceration medical care. The system agreed to rehabilitate me, then it stuck me in an enclosed area with other untreated addicted folks to fantasize about how we would get out and shoot dope the first day (many of us ultimately did, although it took me a couple weeks to get high). The system stripped me naked, took photos and searched inside me. The system threw away letters and photos from my family when they weren't properly stored or mailed in. The system paroled me without preparing me for the world, and predictably, I violated that parole. And the system was more than willing to lock me back up, one of the few things it does incredibly well.

We will always need somewhere to put people when they act up. Very few prison abolitionists envision a world (anytime in the near future) where we never have the need to remove someone from society for a limited time in an effort to protect others. Humans are unpredictable, lust-fueled creatures who love violence and domination, and we are all beholden to biological and emotional experiences which eliminate our agency to act in our own best interests. We sometimes require temporary containment for the protection of others. But the term prison is loaded down with the cultural baggage that comes with centuries of stories describing it as the place where all our nightmares live. The facilities where we ultimately decide to house people who need to be pulled out of the public square should not even slightly resemble the current structure of hard walls and cold bars, of warehousing bodies and ignoring the damage done. If the government took personal property from people and punished it for a limited time, then returned it as beat up and abused as many of us come home from prison, we would immediately update the system to prevent that damage. But incarcerated lives are less important to us than property. We've come a long way in a century of prison film.

The system is *not* broken. You probably noticed that throughout this text I have failed to point out the places where the wheels are falling off, so to speak. In all of my criticism and finger-wagging, I've never discovered a place where smoke is billowing and gears are grinding, a place where the system's paradoxical nature is so extreme that the entire process breaks down. That's because the system operates beautifully, from an engineering perspective at least. It incentivizes bad behavior on both sides of the power hierarchy—those in prison and those paid to supervise them—and then it blames individual actors for their predictable (and preventable) behavior when it's brought to light, rapidly replacing them with new actors who are incentivized the same as everyone else. It dehumanizes us with minimum sentence requirements, jail time for what it claims to believe is a disease (addiction), and high recidivism rates which it continues to ignore. It is designed to uphold the appearance of good faith and attempted rehabilitation, but instead of softening us and preparing us for a life in the free world, it hardens us and provides us with additional traumatic experiences which make it difficult to function once we are released. It is a system of torture, camouflaged in antique rags of good intentions. If it were broken, at least we could just fix it and move on. But it's working just fine. People are collecting checks, punching clocks, moving bodies and warehousing bad guys. Everything appears to be normal as production proceeds unincumbered.

From every angle one looks, the prison system is humming away smoothly, like a well-lubricated factory full of machines tied one to the next. Bodies roll in, they go through the gears and grinders, and they roll out, indelibly changed by the production process they have undergone, yet always blamed for their own behavior, as if they operate in a vacuum. The new correctional system, whenever we get around to building it, will look very different in that the concerns above, which are an obvious element of the current machine of justice, will be deliberately and constantly excluded, pressed out and replaced with updated incentives for those who operate as cogs in the machine; the correctional system will be corrected.

People will always act up, and any rules we make will inevitably (and rapidly) be broken. Those who break the rules sometimes need guidance, but sometimes they need therapy, or medication, or connection, or love (or all of the above). Right now, we have a big stick which is occasionally padded in various nice-sounding names, like drug court, probation and community corrections. But the focus of our so-called justice system remains retribution with a side of restitution. We don't even attempt to prevent the crimes that the court is charged with avenging. Yet we spend billions of dollars attempting to clean up messes left behind when crimes occur, and we spend decades locking people who would otherwise be tax-paying citizens inside expensive prisons. The goal of the new justice system will be prevention and restoration. Yes, people will always break the rules. But if the rules are just, and if the system is designed to incentivize citizenship, participation, equity and second (and third, and fourth, etc.) chances, it will turn out a very different result than the steady 75%(+) recidivism rate (within just five years of release) we have long maintained in the United States.[290]

I end this text with a call for correctional reorientation. Instead of punishment, revenge and restitution, we should focus on prevention, inclusion and community connection. People commit crimes because they are put in positions where they feel those crimes are necessary, or sometimes even ethical. They break the law when they are taught to break the law, or when they feel as if they have no other choice. And those of us who wind up in prison often learn (usually through sources other than prison) to rethink many of the taken-for-granted norms which land us there in the first place. Once those changes are enacted, we naturally attempt to live different lives with different goals. Identity is a huge piece of the puzzle. When we take someone who is in a bad place—bad enough to commit a crime capable of landing them in prison—and we put them into a worse place—prison—we virtually ensure they will spin further down the rabbit hole of bad luck, self-victimization and unresolved trauma. We relabel their rough patch in life as a permanent, defining characteristic, and we replace their name with a number that will stay with them until the day they die. For some of us, the label of outlaw feels nice compared to the labelless life we led prior, so we adopt the identity and spend our time in prison doing one of the only things there is to do—becoming better outlaws.

Once the system is redesigned, instead of locking us down and pushing us away when we get into trouble, society will draw us close and give us what we need to succeed, helping us become stable, contributing members of a society. When I was released from prison in 2005, I found myself briefly living in a world between worlds, a liminal borderland where my identity was constantly up for debate.[291] I had to report to the parole office every week, and I had to take a drug test across town any day that my number came up in a random drawing (around four times each week). I was required to attend community reentry meetings where the teacher would press 12-step spirituality and "follow the rules or else" compliance. And in all of these places I found myself surrounded by people like me, folks who were also stuck between worlds, trying to work out their own identities while finding themselves reminded on a consistent basis that, above all else, we will always be convicted, addicted, restricted people, less worthy than everyone else. Even when those of us who have been to prison rise through the various social systems of hierarchy, like business or academia, we still encounter gatekeepers at every step, double-checking to make sure we have behaved since release, asking us to explain things we did decades ago, on the worst days of our lives, and forcing us to apologize repeatedly . . . forever. And in the end, we often still aren't allowed in some spaces, or we are, but just barely, and with increased oversight. This is not redemption.

I envision a world where we devote a fraction of the time, energy and resources currently aimed at punishment instead to restoration, training, therapy, medication, treatment, job placement, and education. It costs nearly $70,000 to incarcerate someone in New York, slightly less in other states, contributing to a massive $80 billion in spending every year in the US on prisons.[292] That's just a fraction of the $300 billion we spend each year on our entire criminal justice system.[293] And for that price, we are ensured that little education or treatment will be received, and that, once released, those who spend time in prison are likely to return in short order.[294] The *Harvard Political Review* recently published an article reporting that, "37% of incarcerated individuals and 44% of those in jail have been diagnosed with a mental health illness," even though "66% of prisoners reported not receiving any form of mental health care during the full length of their incarceration."[295] Meanwhile, we continue to lock people up for both using and selling drugs despite the fact that most drugs are incredibly cheap to produce from raw materials (around a dollar-per-gram for cocaine and heroin), but more valuable than gold *because* of their illegality.[296] We could end the war on drugs and get rid of *all* illegal drug dealers overnight by legalizing and regulating drugs, sending users to doctors and therapists instead of dealers, and removing the ability of small time suppliers to make a profit. Instead, we continue to arrest addicted people who we claim to believe have a disease, along with "dealers" who are often just selling to pay the rent, or to feed their families (or their habits).

The good news is there is a lot of space for progress, from drug policy to mental health to education and training. Things certainly won't change overnight, and that's probably a good thing, because the system we have built and operated for the last hundred years of punishment has been devoted to ensuring those who abide there have every opportunity to become self-fulfilling prophecies. I did 340 pushups over and over to prepare for the hellhole I knew I was about to enter, and then I got there and realized it was nothing like what I had been told. It isn't packed with shower rapes and knife fights. It isn't grimy guards and a confusing "inmate code" enforced with violence. It's just a place where our culture throws those who it doesn't want to look at. It is cold, lonely, expensive, hierarchical and designed to be disorienting and overwhelming. Of course, when you lock *anyone* in a situation like that, then restrict markers of individuality, media, stimulation, and tools for self-improvement, you are certain to see tensions rise and identities shift. We are humans, so we develop defenses when we are forced to remain in stressful situations. If those outside prison *only* see our defenses on TV or in film, spectaclized for mass audience consumption and distilled into a tight three-minute scene, they might come to believe that's all we are—Hollywood monsters caged for the safety of society. Along with our change of focus as we move toward the new justice system (from punishment to prevention), we will also notice a change in representations, for the current need to hide from ourselves what we are doing to our neighbors will no longer exist, and the veil which currently hides the prison from the public's view will be a thing of the past, along with the media spectacles which work their magic by breaking through that wall. The spectacle and the real will change in unison, updating in the dance of life and art which Plato and Wilde began describing centuries ago. Now let's dance.

> "That's what this is about . . . the same principles as Harriet Tubman: reach to here and bring to here. Legit...all the people you threw away, the dope dealers, the criminals, they will be legit, sitting next to you in first class, thanks to your boy."[297] —Tupac Shakur

Notes

1. Michelle Alexander, *The New Jim Crow: Mass Incarceration in the Age of Colorblindness* (New York: The New Press, 2010/2012).
2. Travis Dixon, "Teaching You to Love Fear: Television News in a Punishing Democracy," in *Challenging the Media Incarceration Complex: Activism & Educational Alternatives,* ed. Stephen Hartnett, (106-123); quote from 114.
3. Laura Kipnis, *Against Love: A Polemic* (New York: Random House, 2003), 185-186.
4. bell hooks describes her work as cultural criticism in the introduction of *Feminism is for Everybody: Passionate Politics* (Cambridge, MA: South End Press, 2000).
5. Theodor Adorno & Max Horkheimer, *Dialectic of Enlightenment,* English translation by John Cumming (New York: Seabury Press, 1977; originally published in 1947), 139.
6. Walter Benjamin, "The Work of Art in the Age of Mechanical Reproduction," in *Illuminations,* edited by Hannah Arendt, translated by Harry Zohn, 1935.
7. Michel de Certeau, *The Practice of Everyday Life* (Berkeley, CA: University of California Press, 1984), 188.
8. bell hooks, "Seeing and Making Culture: Representing the Poor," in *Outlaw Culture: Resisting Representations* (New York: Routledge, 1994).
9. bell hooks, "Introduction: Making Movie Magic," in *Reel to Real: Race, Class and Sex at the Movies* (New York: Routledge, 1996/2009), 12.
10. Travis Dixon, "Good Guys Are Still Always in White? Positive Change and Continued Misrepresentation of Race and Crime on Local Television News," *Communication Research 44,* (6): 2017.
11. Bill Yousman, "Challenging the Media-Incarceration Complex through Media-Education," in *Working for Justice: A Handbook of Prison Education and Activism,* ed. Stephen J. Hartnett et al. (Chicago, IL: University of Illinois Press, 2013): 141-160.
12. Kathleen Donovan and Charles Klahm IV, "The Role of Entertainment Media in Perceptions of Police Use of Force," *Criminal Justice and Behavior 42,* (12): 2015.
13. Allison Page and Laurie Ouellette, "The Prison-Television Complex." *International Journal of Cultural Studies 23:* (1), 2020: 133.
14. Both Bill Yousman and Travis Dixon (above) found similar results that went unnoticed by participants.
15. Matt Miller, Dom Nero and Brady Langmann, "*No Way Home* is Good, but not the Best Spiderman Movie Ever," *Esquire,* December 17, 2021.
16. bell hooks, "Introduction: Making Movie Magic," in *Reel to Real: Race, Class and Sex at the Movies* (New York: Routledge, 1996/2009), 12.
17. Michelle Brown, *The Culture of Punishment: Prison, Society and Spectacle* (New York University Press, 2009), 4.
18. Carl Jung, *On the Nature of the Psyche* (New York, NY: Dell-Random House, 1947), 417.
19. *Les Misérables,* directed by Tom Hooper (2012; Universal City, CA: Universal Studios, 2012). Original story written in 1845.

20. Susan Wioszczyna, "Merciless Critics Lead the 'Les Mis' Rebellion," *USA Today,* January 24, 2013. The Internet Movie Database keeps detailed records of movie casts, producers, rights, and awards won at http://www.imdb.com

21. Manohla Dargis, "The Wretched Lift Their Voices: 'Les Misérables' Stars Anne Hathaway and Hugh Jackman," *New York Times,* December 24, 2012.

22. *Les Misérables*, directed by J. Stuart Blackton (Vitagraph Company of America, 1909).

23. Carl Jung, *Man and his Symbols* (New York, NY: Dell-Random House Publishing, 1964), 58.

24 Batman's Robin, *Harry Potter's* Ron Weasley, *Independence Day's* David Levinson, *Animaniacs'* Pinky.

25 *Dangerous Minds,* Louanne Johnson (Michelle Pfeiffer), *Dead Poet's Society's* John Keating (Robin Williams), *School of Rock's* Dewey Finn (Jack Back), *X-Men's* Professor Xavier.

26 Walt Disney Productions, *Sleeping Beauty* (1959) contains a scene where the main character, Sleeping Beauty, it kissed by a prince and brought back to life. ABC, *The Wonder Years* (1968-1973) was based on a young boy's infatuation for his neighbor and best friend. It was rebooted in 2021 and contained a magic kiss scene in the second season. 20th Century Studio's *Free Guy* (2021) contained a magic kiss scene with the main character.

27. Aniela Jaffé, "Sacred Symbols: The Stone and the Animal," in *Man and his Symbols,* ed. Carl Jung (Aldus Books, 1964; reprinted by Random House, 1968), 257.

28 The film versions vary from one another. For example, the 1978 version depicted Valjean escaping from Toulon Prison, not gaining his parole, and he spends his life fleeing from the original charges, whereas the 2012 version depicts Valjean break-ing his parole and creating a new identity in response to the gift of silver.

29 Various alternative starting points have been toyed with in different versions of films, including one where Valjean escapes instead of being paroled. The original novel begins with his parole, not his escape.

30 Victor Hugo, *Les Misérables* (New York, NY: Penguin Group, 1987).

31. Mike Nellis, "The Aesthetics of Redemption: Released Prisoners in American Film and Literature," *Theoretical Criminology* 13, no. 1 (2009): 129-146, quotation at 131.

32. Nellis, "The Aesthetics of Redemption," 132.

33. Nellis, "The Aesthetics of Redemption," 132.

34. Samuel Bischoff (director), *The Last Mile,* (KBS Productions, 1932). Another edition of the film starring Micky Rooney was released in 1959. For US TV sets in the 1940s, see Matthew Wilson, "How TVs Have Changed Through the Decades," *Business Insider,* January 17, 2020.

35. *The Count of Monte Cristo* was rebooted again, most recently in 2002. The 1934 version was directed by Rowland Lee (United States: Reliance Pictures, 1934).

36. *Convict's Code,* directed by Lambert Hillyer (Crescent Pictures Corp., 1939).

37. *Castle on the Hudson*, directed by Anatole Litvak (New York: Warner Brothers, 1940).

38. *Jail House Rock,* directed by Richard Thorpe, (Metro-Goldwyn-Mayer, 1957).

39. *Birdman of Alcatraz,* directed by John Frankenheimer, (United Artists, 1962). "'Birdman of Alcatraz' Film Draws Praise from Critics," in *Eugene Register-Guard,* May 13, 1962.

40. *Cool Hand Luke*, directed by Stuart Rosenberg (Burbank, CA: Warner Brothers-Seven Arts, 2008).

41. *The Dirty Dozen,* directed by Robert Aldrich (1967, Los Angeles, CA: Metro-Goldwyn-Mayer, 2000).

42. The Hollywood Foreign Press Association keeps records of awards on their website, www.goldenblobes.org

43. *The Longest Yard,* directed by Robert Aldrich (1974, Hollywood, CA: Paramount Pictures, 2005).

44. *Escape from Alcatraz,* directed by Don Siegel (1979, San Francisco, CA: Paramount Pictures, 2013).

45. Roger Ebert, review of *Escape from Alcatraz,* June 27, 1979.

46. One of the sub-plots used in *The Shawshank Redemption* involves Red's repeated visits to the parole board, where every ten years he is allowed to pour his heart out and beg for a second chance. He is denied over and over, despite what appear to be legitimate claims of having made a mistake as a kid and worked to better himself. But in the end, as an old man, he gives up and is eventually freed when he tells the parole board "I don't really give a shit."

47. Nellis, "The Aesthetics of Redemption," 136.

48. *Sling Blade,* directed by Billy Bob Thornton (1996, New York, NY: Miramax Films, 2001).

49. John Goldwyn Productions, CBS Television, *Dexter* has now joined the ranks of reboots, originally produced from 2006-2013, then resigned for 2022 as *Dexter: New Blood.* Dexter is a detective who commits murders when he discovers bad guys who can't be stopped any other way. As of this writing, there are three seasons of HBO's *Barry,* a TV show about a contract killer who discovers acting.

50. *The Rock,* directed by Michael Bay (1996, CA: Hollywood Pictures).

51. Janet Maslin, "American History X: Film Review: The Darkest Chambers of a Nation's Soul," *New York Times,* October 28, 1998.

52. *American History X,* directed by Tony Kaye (1998, New York, NY: New Line Cinema, 1999).

53. Helen Eigenberg & Agnes Baro, "If you Drop the Soap in the Shower you are on your own: Images of Male Rape in Selected Prison Movies," *Sexuality and Culture* 7, (4): Dec, 2003, 56-66. Quotation at page 76.

54. *Life,* directed by Ted Demme (Hollywood, CA: Imagine Entertainment, 1999).

55. *Oh Brother, Where Art Thou?* directed by Joel Coen (Hollywood, CA: Universal Pictures, 2000).

56. *The Last Castle,* directed by Rod Lurie (Nashville, TV: Robert Lawrence Productions, 2001).

57. One of the earliest and most popular tropes of sacrificing one's life to save another is Christianity's Jesus.

58. *Conviction,* directed by Kevin Sullivan (Hollywood, CA: Paramount, 2002).

59. *Get Rich or Die Tryin',* directed by Jim Sheridan (Hollywood, CA: Paramount Pictures, 2006).

60. Nellis, "The Aesthetics of Redemption," 140.

61. *Prison Break,* created by Paul Scheuring (2005-2009 & 2017, Los Angeles, CA: 20th Century Fox Television, 2006).

62. *Let's Go to Prison!* produced by Marc Abraham, (Carsey Warner, 2006).

63. *I Love you Phillip Morris,* directed by John Requa and Glenn Ficarra, (LD Entertainment, 2009).

64. *Stone,* produced by John Curran, (2010, Las Angeles, CA: Mimran Pictures).

65. Charles Bright, *The Powers that Punish: Prison and Politics in the Era of the 'Big House', 1920-1955* (Ann Arbor: University of Michigan Press: 1996).

66. *Orange is the New Black,* created by Jenji Kohan, (2013-2019, New York: Lions Gate Television)..

67. Suzanne Enck and Megan Morrissey, "If Orange is the New Black, I must be Colorblind: Comic Framings of Post-Racism in the Prison-Industrial Complex," *Critical Studies in Media Communication 32,* (5): 2015.

68. Suzanne Enck and Megan Morrissey, "If Orange is the New Black, I must be Colorblind."

69. Terry Gross & Jenji Kohan (quote from Kohan), *Fresh Air* on NPR, "'Orange' Creator Jenji Kohan: 'Piper was my Trojan Horse'," August 13, 2013.

70. *Weeds,* created by Jenji Kohan (New York: Showtime, 2005-2013). Prison scenes in Season 7, Episode 1.

71. *Escape Plan,* directed by Mikael Håfström, (Summit Entertainment, 2013).

72. *Escape Plan 2,* directed by Steven Miller, (Summit Entertainment, 2018).

73. *Papillon,* directed by Michael Noer, (Siberia: Red Granite Pictures, 2017).

74. *Corrective Measures,* directed by Sean O'Reilly (TUBI, 2022).

75. Carl Jung, *Man and his Symbols,* 58.

76. Yousman, "Challenging the Media-Incarceration Complex," 146.

77. Marshall McLuhan and Quentin Fiore, *The Medium is the Massage: An Inventory of Effects* (Berkely, CA: Gingko Press, Inc., 1967), 8.

78. Of course, 4% is a shameful number, but think about how often you see sexual assault in prison film. It's more than 4%. US Department of Justice: Bureau of Justice Statistics, "PREA Data Collection Activities, 2021," (June, 2021): NCJ 300438.

79. bell hooks, "Power to the Pussy: We Don't Wanna Be Dicks in Drag," in *Outlaw Culture: Resisting Representations* (New York: Routledge Press, 1994), 16.

80. Helen Eigenberg & Agnes Baro, "If you Drop the Soap in the Shower you are on your own: Images of Male Rape in Selected Prison Movies," *Sexuality and Culture 7,* (2003), 86, 64.

81. Dawn K. Cecil, "Looking Beyond Caged Heat: Media Images of Women in Prison," *Feminist Criminology* 2 (2007): 304-326, quotation at 305.

82. Leonidas K. Cheliotis, "The Ambivalent Consequences of Visibility: Crime and Prisons in the Mass Media," *Crime, Media, Culture* 6 (2010): 169-184, quotation at 175.

83. Understandably, many of us cannot travel to the space of prison film without experiencing trauma. Those who already have trauma in their past are often triggered by violent representations of prison, and those on the autism spectrum, like me, often struggle to turn off the portions of our brain responsible for empathy, causing such depictions to feel personal and taxing.

84. Cheliotis, "The Ambivalent Consequences of Visibility," 175.

85. *Goodfellas,* directed by Martin Scorsese (Hollywood, CA: Warner Brothers, 1990). *Suicide Squad,* directed by David Ayer (Hollywood, CA: Warner Brothers, 2016).

86. Michel de Certeau, *The Practice of Everyday Life* (Berkeley, CA: University of California Press, 1984), 187.

87. Yousman, "Challenging the Media-Incarceration Complex," 152.

88. bell hooks, "Introduction: Making Movie Magic," in *Reel to Real: Race, Class and Sex at the Movies* (New York: Routledge, 1996/2009), 3.

89. See The Bible New International Version, Matthew 14:6-12.

90. See Leviticus 24:16 for blasphemy; see Leviticus 20:10 for adultery; see Leviticus 20:13 for homosexuality.

91. Numbers 15:34, Deuteronomy 17:2-7, Leviticus 24:10-16.

92. As an example, the Jesus of the New Testament once prevented a woman from being stoned for adultery by pointing to the sins of the stone-throwers: "let he who is without sin cast the first stone," John 8:7.

93. Michel Foucault, *Discipline and Punish: The Birth of the Prison,* (New York: Vintage Books, 1995).

94. Sigmund Freud, *Civilization and its Discontents* (Blacksburg, Virginia: Wilder Publications, 2010), 59.

95. Michelle Alexander, *The New Jim Crow: Mass Incarceration in the Age of Colorblindness* (New York: The New Press, 2010/2012), 139.

96. Michel Foucault, *Discipline and Punish: The Birth of the Prison,* (New York: Vintage Books, 1995), 3-6.

97. Stephen J. Hartnett, *Executing Democracy Volume One: Capital Punishment & the Making of America 1683-1807* (East Lansing, MI: Michigan State University Press, 2010), 49.

98. Christine Harold and Kevin DeLuca, "Behold the Corpse: Violent Images and the Case of Emmett Till," *Rhetoric & Public Affairs 8,* (5): 2005, 268.

99. Foucault, *Discipline and Punish,* 19.

100. Slave labor was not only frequently used as "punishment" in post-Civil War USA, but it is also an ongoing issue in prisons and jails across the country today.

101. Max Weber, "Politics as a Vocation," speech given to "Free Students Union" in Munich, 1919.

102. This gem of a scene is from the cable television series *Oz,* created by Tom Fontana (HBO Studios, 1997-2003) Season 1, Episode 1.

103 Michelle Brown, *The Culture of Punishment: Prison, Society and Spectacle* (New York University Press, 2009), 5.

104. Prison Population numbers from Roy Walmsley, "World Prison Population List: 12th Edition," *World Prison Brief,* (Institute for Criminal Policy Research). Budget numbers from The Urban Institute, State and Local Finances Initiative, "Criminal Justice Expenditures: Police, Corrections, and Courts," accessed 1/29/22.

105. Liz Benecchi, "Recidivism Imprisons American Progress," *Harvard Political Review,* August 8, 2021.

106. Ray Surette, *Media, Crime, and Criminal Justice: Images and Realities* (Pacific Grove, CA: Cole Publishing, 1992), 1.

107. Angela McRobbie and Sarah Thornton, "Rethinking 'Moral Panic' for Multi-Mediated Social Worlds," *British Journal of Sociology 46,* (4): (1995), 571.

108. Guy Debord, *Society of the Spectacle* (Detroit, MI: Black & Red, 1983), 177.

109. Walter Benjamin, ed. Hannah Arendt, *The Work of Art in the Mechanical Age of Reproduction* (New York: Random House, 1936), section II.

110. bell hooks, "Good Girls Look the Other Way," in *Reel to Real: Race, Class and Sex at the Movies* (New York: Routledge, 1996/2009), 13.

111. Theodor Adorno & Max Horkheimer, *Dialectic of Enlightenment,* English translation by John Cumming (New York: Seabury Press, 1977; originally published in 1947), 139.

112. Michelle Brown, *The Culture of Punishment: Prison, Society and Spectacle* (New York University Press, 2009), 4.

113. Cheliotis, "The Ambivalent Consequences of Visibility," 174.

114. The "culture industry" is a reference to the work of Theodor Adorno and Max Horkheimer in "The Culture Industry: Enlightenment as Mass Deception," in *Dialectics of Enlightenment.*

115. bell hooks, "Whose Pussy is it Anyway?" in *Reel to Real: Race, Class and Sex at*

the *Movies* (New York: Routledge, 1996/2009), 292.

116. Christine Harold and Kevin DeLuca, "Behold the Corpse: Violent Images and the Case of Emmett Till," *Rhetoric & Public Affairs 8*, (5), 265.

117. Michel de Certeau, *The Practice of Everyday Life* (Berkeley, CA: University of California Press, 1984), 187.

118. Shawshank Prison is the setting of a short story originally published in: Stephen King, *Different Seasons* (New York, NY: Viking Press, 1982). The short story was adapted into a movie: *The Shawshank Redemption, w*ritten and directed by Frank Darabont (1995, Culver City, CA: Columbia Pictures, 1999).

119. Certeau, *The Practice of Everyday Life,* 187.

120. bell hooks, "Doing it for Daddy: Black Masculinity in the Mainstream," in *Reel to Real: Race, Class and Sex at the Movies* (New York: Routledge, 1996/2009), 110.

121. Adorno & Horkheimer, *Dialectic of Enlightenment,* 126.

122. Plato, *The Republic* (Norwalk, CT: The Easton Press, 1944), 529. Written in the fourth century B.C.

123. Oscar Wilde, "The Decay of Lying: An Observation," in *Intentions* (Public Domain Work, Project Gutenberg Ebook, 1997). Originally published in 1891.

124. Fredric Jameson, *Postmodernism, or, the Cultural Logic of Late Capitalism* (North Carolina: Duke University Press, 1991), 24.

125. bell hooks, "Introduction: Making Movie Magic," in *Reel to Real: Race, Class and Sex at the Movies* (New York: Routledge, 1996/2009), 2.

126. *The Birth of a Nation* was originally a book by Thomas Dixon Jr. called *The Clansman,* written in 1905. The film version was directed by D. W. Griffith and released in 1915.

127. Cheliotis, "The Ambivalent Consequences of Visibility," 175.

128. Travis L. Dixon, "Teaching You to Love Fear: Television News and Racial Stereotypes in a Punishing Democracy," in *Challenging the Prison Industrial Complex: Activism, Arts & Educational Alternatives,* ed. by Stephen J. Hartnett (Chicago, IL: University of Illinois Press, 2011), 107-123, quote from 114.

129. Sue Mahan & Richard Lawrence, "Media and Mayhem in Corrections: The Role of the Media in Prison Riots," *The Prison Journal* 76 (1996): 420-441, quotations at 420, 423.

130. He went on to say, "It must have scope. Yet it must also possess simplicity, in that it is broadly a reduction of the subject matter." Kenneth Burke, *A Grammar of Motives* (Berkeley, CA: University of California Press, 1945), 60.

131. Burke, *A Grammar of Motives,* 59.

132. Michelle Brown, *The Culture of Punishment: Prison, Society and Spectacle* (New York University Press, 2009), 5.

133. Steven Shaviro, *Post Cinematic Affect* (Washington: O Books, 2010), 93.

134. Shaviro, *Post Cinematic Affect,* 2-3.

135. Guy Debord, *Society of the Spectacle* (Detroit, MI: Black & Red, 1983), 42.

136. Debord, *Society of the Spectacle,* 47.

137. Yousman, "Challenging the Media-Incarceration Complex," 152. "Referential reality" from Michel de Certeau, *The Practice of Everyday Life.*

138. Yousman, "Challenging the Media-Incarceration Complex," 146.

139. Nicole Fleetwood, *Marking Time: Art in the Age of Mass Incarceration* (Cambridge, MA: Harvard University Press, 2020), 15.

140. bell hooks, "Introduction: Making Movie Magic," in *Reel to Real: Race, Class and Sex at the Movies* (New York: Routledge, 1996/2009), 1.

141. Walter Benjamin, "The Work of Art in the Age of Mechanical Reproduction,"

Section IV, in *Illuminations,* edited by Hannah Arendt, translated by Harry Zohn, 1935.

142. *Prison Break, c*reated by Paul Scheuring (2005-2009 & 2017, Los Angeles, CA: 20th Century Fox Television).

143. 2006 People's Choice Awards results at http://www.peopleschoice.com

144. Robert Bianco, "'Prison Break' Debut has Lock on Suspense," *USA Today,* August 28, 2005.

145. Sheuring, "Pilot," *Prison Break,* 2005.

146. Sheuring, "Riots, Drills, and the Devil (Part I)," *Prison Break,* 2005.

147. Sheuring, S1E2, "Allen," *Prison Break,* 2005.

148. Jennifer Schneider, Jackson Bosley, Glenn Ferguson and Merrill Main, "The Challenges of Sexual Offense Treatment Programs in Correctional Facilities," *The Journal of Psychiatry & Law 34,* (Summer, 2006).

149. Kevin Steinmetz and Don Kurtz, "Masculinity in *It's Always Sunny in Philadelphia,*" in *Crime TV: Streaming Criminology in Popular Culture,* eds. Jonathan Grubb and Chad Posick (New York University Press, 2021), 232.

150. Sheuring, "Riots, Drills, and the Devil (Parts I& II)," *Prison Break,* September 25 & October 3, 2005.

151. bell hooks, "Introduction: Making Movie Magic," in *Reel to Real: Race, Class and Sex at the Movies* (New York: Routledge, 1996/2009), 4.

152. Brian Myers, "Friends with Benefits: Plausible Optimism and the Practice of Teabagging in Video Games," *Games and Culture 14,* (7-8), 2019: 763-780.

153. *The Shawshank Redemption,* written and directed by Frank Darabont (1995, Culver City, CA: Columbia Pictures).

154. *Oz,* created by Tom Fontana Bayonne (1997-2003, New Jersey: Levinson/Fontana Company & HBO, 2004).

155. Elayne Rapping, *Law and Justice as Seen on TV* (New York: University Press, 2003), 81.

156. Bill Yousman, "Inside *Oz:* Hyperviolence, Race and Class Nightmares, and the Engrossing Spectacle of Terror," *Communication and Critical/Cultural Studies 6,* (3): 2009.

157. Yousman, "Challenging the Media-Incarceration Complex," 147.

158. Bill Yousman, "Inside *Oz*: Hyperviolence, Race and Class Nightmares, and the Engrossing Spectacle of Terror," *Communication and Critical/Cultural Studies 6* (September, 2009), 265-284, quote at 267.

159. Sheuring, "Cell Test" & "Flight," *Prison Break,* September 5, 2005 & May 15, 2006.

160. *Goodfellas,* directed by Martin Scorsese (1990, Beverly Hills, CA: Warner Brothers Studios). *The Sopranos,* created by David Chase (1999 – 2007, USA: HBO Studios).

161. Sheuring, "Pilot," *Prison Break,* August 29, 2005.

162. Sheuring, "Cute Poison," *Prison Break,* September 12, 2005.

163. Sheuring, "End of the Tunnel," *Prison Break,* November 28, 2005.

164. *Fate of the Furious, F8, Fast and Furious 8* (all titles used in the film) directed by F. Gary Grey (Hollywood, CA: Universal Studies, 2017)

165. Sigmund Freud, *Wit and its Relation to the Unconscious* (New York: Moffat, Yard and Company, 1916), 147, 193-194.

166. Steven Shaviro, *Post Cinematic Affect* (United Kingdom: O Books, 2010), 118.

167. From the documentary series *George Carlin's American Dream,* episode 2, directed by Judd Apatow (2022, USA: HBO Max).

168. *Oz,* HBO.

169. Sigmund Freud, *Wit and its Relation to the Unconscious* (New York, NY: Moffat, Yard and Company, 1916), 206, 150.

170. Andrea Samson and James Gross, "Humour as Emotional Regulation: The Differential Consequences of Negative Versus Positive Humour," *Cognition and Emotion 26,* (2): 2012.

171. Kenneth Burke, *Attitudes Toward History, 3rd edition,* (Berkeley: University of California Press, 1937/1984).

172. Kenneth Burke, *Attitudes Toward History, 3rd edition,* 39.

173. Burke, *Attitudes Toward History,* 41.

174. A. Cheree Carlson, "Limitations on the Comic Frame: Some Witty American Women of the Nineteenth Century," *Quarterly Journal of Speech, 74,* (3), 1988, p. 312.

175. Carlson, "Limitations on the Comic Frame," 312.

176. Carlson, "Limitations on the Comic Frame," 312.

177. *Up In Smoke,* directed by Steve Adler (1978, Los Angeles, CA: Paramount Pictures).

178. Federal Bureau of Prisons, "Inmate Handbook," Springfield, MO: Federal Bureau of Prisons, 2012) 68. State facilities generally enforce similar rules prohibiting any sort of sexual activity or cohabitation of spaces, including bunks.

179. *Anger Management,* created by Bruce Helford (2012-2014, Los Angeles, CA: Joe Roth Television, 2013).

180. *Rolling Stone,* "Charlie Sheen's 'Anger Management' Breaks Ratings Record," June 29, 2012.

181. Qing Cai, Sinead Chen, et. al., "Modulation of Humor Rating of Bad Jokes by Other People's Laughter," *Current Biology 28,* (14), 2019.

182. Helford, "Charlie and the Prison Riot," *Anger Management,* August 15, 2013.

183. *Life,* directed by Ted Demme (1999, Universal City, CA: Universal Studios, 1999). See also Roger Ebert, review of *Life,* April 16, 1999.

184. *The Shawshank Redemption.*

185. *Lets Go to Prison,* directed by Bod Odenkirk (2006, Universal City, CA: Universal Studios, 2007).

186. Neil Genzlinger, "Prison Comedy with a Shank, not an Ax," *New York Times,* November 18, 2006.

187. Bill Yousman, "Inside *Oz:* Hyperviolence, Race and Class Nightmares, and the Engrossing Spectacle of Terror," *Communication and Critical/Cultural Studies,* (August 2009).

188. Dreama Moon, "White Enculturation and Bourgeois Ideology: The Discursive Production of "Good (White) Girls," in Martin & Nakayama (editors.), *Whiteness: The Social Communication of Identity* (177–197) (Newbury Park, CA: Sage Press, 1999).

189. Certeau, *The Practice of Everyday Life,* 187.

190. Rapping, *Law and Justice as Seen on TV,* 81.

191. Yousman, "Challenging the Media-Incarceration Complex," 146.

192. *Prison Break,* Season 1, episode 1.

193. Elvis Mitchell, review of *Animal Factory,* "Surviving the Lockup One Way or Another," *New York Times,* October 20, 2000.

194. *Animal Factory,* directed by Steve Buscemi (2000, Philadelphia, PA: Franchise Pictures, 2002).

195. Roger Ebert, review of *Blood in, Blood out: Bound by Honor,* April 30, 1993.

196. *Blood In Blood out: Bound by Honor,* directed by Taylor Hackford (1993, Hollywood, CA: Hollywood Pictures, 2001).

197. Eigenberg & Baro, "If you Drop the Soap in the Shower you are on your own," 87.

198. *Oz,* created by Tom Fontana, (HBO, 1997-2003).

199. Erica R. Meiners, "Life after *Oz:* Ignorance, Mass Media, and Making Public Enemies," *Review of Education, Pedagogy, and Cultural Studies 29,* (1): 2007.

200. "The Rose that Grew From Concrete" is a poem attributed to Tupac Shakur, and an idea he frequently discussed, including in a 1996 interview on the set of the film *Gridlock'd* which is still available on multiple websites.

201. Nicole Fleetwood, *Marking Time: Art in the Age of Mass Incarceration* (Cambridge, MA: Harvard University Press, 2020), 16.

202. Guy Debord, *Society of the Spectacle* (Detroit, MI: Black & Red, 1983), 1, 4.

203. Julia Keller, "Stephen King: AWOL from his own Biography," *The Chicago Tribune,* January 11, 2009.

204. Cheliotis, "The Ambivalent Consequences of Visibility," 175.

205. Nellis, "The Aesthetics of Redemption," 132.

206. *The Green Mile,* written and directed by Frank Darabont (1999, Burbank, CA: Warner Brothers Entertainment Inc., 2007). Roger Ebert, review of *The Green Mile,* December 10, 1999.

207. Eigenberg & Baro, "If you Drop the Soap in the Shower," 76.

208. Eigenberg & Baro, "If you Drop the Soap in the Shower," 87.

209. *Short Eyes,* directed by Robert M. Young (1977, New York, NY: Film League, uploaded 2013).

210. Vincent Canby, review of *Short Eyes,* "Film 'Short Eyes' Eloquently Adapted," *New York Times,* September 28, 1977.

211. *Con Air,* directed by Simon West (1997, Burbank, CA: Disney-Touchstone Pictures, 1999).

212. Janet Maslin, review of *Con Air,* "Signs and Symbols on a Thrill Ride," *New York Times,* June 6, 1997.

213. Of course, Andy wasn't guilty in *The Shawshank Redemption.* But we don't know this until the film plays out. John Grisham's novel, *A Time to Kill,* was scripted and filmed as a movie released in1996. It is centered on a father's decision to kill his daughter's rapists after the courts fail to imprison them.

214. Rapping, *Law and Justice as Seen on TV,* 81.

215. Sean O'Sullivan, "Representing 'The Killing State': The Death Penalty in Nineties Hollywood Cinema," *The Howard Journal 42,* (5): December, 2003, 490.

216. John Sloop, *The Culture Prison: Discourse, Prisoners, and Punishment* (Tuscaloosa, AL: The University of Alabama Press, 1996), 145.

217. A. O. Scott, review of *Monster's Ball,* "Courtesy and Decency Play Sneaky With a Tough Guy," *New York Times,* December 26, 2001.

218. *Monster's Ball,* directed by Marc Forster (2001, Vancouver, British Columbia: Lions Gate Films, 2002).

219. Certeau, *The Practice of Everyday Life,* 187.

220. Samuel Bischoff (director), *The Last Mile,* (KBS Productions, 1932).

221. *Con Air.*

222. Yousman, "Challenging the Media-Incarceration Complex," 146.

223. *The Green Mile.*

224. Hannah Arendt, *A Report on the Banality of Evil: Eichmann in Jerusalem* (New York, NY: Penguin Books, 1965), 276.

225. Arendt, *A Report on the Banality of Evil,* 276.

226. *Dead Man Walking,* directed by Tim Robbins (1995, Universal City, CA: PolyGram Filmed Entertainment, 2013).

227. Leonardo Antenangeli and Matthew Durose, "Recidivism of Prisoners Released in 24 States in 2008: A Ten-Year Follow-up Period (2008-2018)," published by US Department of Justice: Bureau of Justice Statistics, (September, 2021).

228. bell hooks, "Introduction: Making Movie Magic," in *Reel to Real: Race, Class and Sex at the Movies* (New York: Routledge, 1996/2009), 2.

229. Michelle Brown, *The Culture of Punishment: Prison, Society and Spectacle* (New York University Press, 2009), 2.

230. Sheuring, S1E2, "Allen," *Prison Break,* 2005.

231. Bill Yousman, "Inside *Oz*: Hyperviolence, Race and Class Nightmares, and the Engrossing Spectacle of Terror," *Communication and Critical/Cultural Studies 6* (September, 2009), 265-284. Commercial downloaded from YouTube 5/14/22 at: https://www.youtube.com/watch?v=ZG2eDH3_zyM

232. Leon Neyfakh, "How to Go to Jail: The Surprisingly Robust Genre of Prison Survival Guides," *Slate,* February 15, 2015.

233. Red from *The Shawshank Redemption* was released only when he claimed he stopped trying to convince them he wanted to leave.

234. Richard Davies, "From Pecan Pralines to 'Dots' as Currency: How the Prison Economy Works," *The Guardian,* August 30, 2019.

235. Bosley Crowther, review of *Cool Hand Luke, New York Times,* November 2, 1967.

236. *Cool Hand Luke.*

237. Foucault, *Discipline and Punish,* 201.

238. Foucault, *Discipline and Punish,* 201.

239. *The Green Mile*

240. Yousman, "Challenging the Media-Incarceration Complex," 146.

241. Meghan Mitchell, David Pyrooz and Scott Decker, "Culture in Prison, Culture on the Street: The Convergence Between the Convict Code and Code of the Street," *Journal of Crime and Justice 44,* (2): 2021.

242. "Belly of the Beast" is a reference to Jack Abbott's 1981 autobiographical prison story, *In the Belly of the Beast.*

243. Perry M. Johnson, *Jackson: The Rise and Fall of the World's Largest Walled Prison* (U.S.A.: Perry M. Johnson, 2014).

244. From *Discourses of Deception: (Re)Examining America's War on Drugs,* (dissertation: ProQuest, 2018).

245. Michelle Brown, *The Culture of Punishment: Prison, Society and Spectacle* (New York: New York University Press, 2009), 63.

246. Nellis, "The Aesthetics of Redemption," 144.

247. Perry Johnson, *Jackson: The Rise and Fall of the World's Largest Walled Prison* (Michigan, Perry Johnson: 2014).

248. Benjamin Boyce, *Dr. Junkie: One Man's Story of Addiction and Crime that will Challenge Everything you Know about the War on Drugs* (Baltimore, MA: Loyola Press, 2022).

249. Yousman, "Challenging the Media-Incarceration Complex," 155.

250. Joseph A. Kirby, "From Death Row, Ex-reporter Seeks Public Support, New Trial," *Chicago Tribune,* July 28, 1995.

251. Timothy Williams, "Execution Case Dropped Against Abu-Jamal," *New York Times,* December 7, 2011.

252. Sara Rimer, "Death Sentence Overturned in 1981 Killing of Officer," *New York Times,* December 19, 2001.

253. Mumia Abu-Jamal, *Live From Death Row* (New York: Avon,1995), 6.

254. Abu-Jamal, *Live From Death Row,* 54.

255. Ted Conover, *New Jack: Guarding Sing Sing* (New York: Random House, 2001); quote taken from front cover.

256. Conover, *New Jack,* 17.

257. Conover, *New Jack,* 21.

258. Conover, *New Jack,* 171.

259. Conover, *New Jack,* 30.

260. Conover, *New Jack,* 295.

261. Conover, *New Jack,* 306.

262. This term, "New Digital Commons," has picked up steam in podcasting communities, but the first time I know of it being used was by Sam Harris in his *Making Sense* podcast.

263. "Doctor" (PhD) and "Junkie" are two powerful labels applied to my name which have opened and closed more doors than I ever would have imagined. As an addicted person, I chose that name for the podcast and the book in an attempt to reappropriate and disable the term junkie.

264. Judith Tannenbaum, *Disguised as a Poem: My Years Teaching Poetry at San Quentin* (Boston: Northeaster University Press, 2000), quote taken from back cover.

265. Tannenbaum, *Disguised as a Poem*, 147.

266. Tannenbaum, *Disguised as a Poem,* 18.

267. Tannenbaum, *Disguised as a Poem,* 140-141.

268. Alan Yuhas, "It's Time to Revisit the Satanic Panic," *The New York Times,* March 31, 2021.

269. Damien Echols, *Life After Death* (New York: Blue Rider Press, 2012), 14.

270. Echols, *Life After Death,* 64-65.

271. Echols, *Life After Death,* 151.

272. Emily Widra, "No Escape: The Trauma of Witnessing Violence in Prison," *Prison Policy Initiative,* December 2, 2020.

273. Stephen J. Hartnett, *Incarceration Nation: Investigative Prison Poems of Hope and Terror* (New York, NY: Rowman & Littlefield Publishers, Inc., 2003), 28.

274. Amos Rogers, "My Prison," in *Captured Words Free Thoughts* volume 9, Fall 20011: ed. Stephen J. Hartnett.

275. Stephen Hartnett (editor), *Challenging the Prison Industrial Complex: Activism, Arts & Educational Alternatives* (Champaign, IL: University of Illinois Press, 2010).

276. "What We Do," Free Press website, http://www.freepress.net

277. Marshall McLuhan and Quentin Fiore, *The Medium is the Massage: An Inventory of Effects* (Berkely, CA: Gingko Press, Inc., 1967).

278. Abu-Jamal, *Live From Death Row,* 104.

279. Conover, *New Jack,* 287.

280. Stephen Hartnett, "Op-Ed: Higher Education will Offer Colorado Prisoners a Second Chance," *Denver Post,* March 3, 2022.

281. Stephen Hartnett, "Communication, Social Justice and Joyful Commitment," *Western Journal of Communication 74,* (1): 2010.

282. Lois M. Davis, Robert Bozick, Jennifer L. Steele, et al., "Evaluating the Effectiveness of Correctional Education: A Meta-Analysis of Programs that Provide Education," to Incarcerated Adults (Santa Monica, CA: RAND Corporation, 2013), 32.

283. VERA Institute, "Second Change Pell Experimental Sites Initiative Update," June

2018.

284. Michelle Alexander, *The New Jim Crow: Mass Incarceration in the Age of Colorblindness* (New York: The New Press, 2010).

285. For Lincoln's stance on slavery, see his speech in Peoria, IL in Autumn 1854, where he expressed his uncertainty about what to do and floated the idea of sending all US slaves to Liberia. See also Ta-Nehisi Coates, "What this Cruel War was Over," *The Atlantic,* June 22, 2015. For missing rights, see *The United States Constitution.*

286. Mumia Abu-Jamal, *Live From Death Row* (New York: Avon Books, 1995/1996), 52.

287. Lori Pompa, "Breaking Down the Walls: Inside-Out Learning and the Pedagogy of Transformation," in *Challenging the Prison-Industrial Complex: Activism, Arts & Educational Alternatives,* ed. Stephen Hartnett, (Urbana, IL: University of Illinois Press, 2011): 253-272, quote from 253.

288. Mumia Abu-Jamal, *Live From Death Row* (New York: Avon Books, 1995/1996), 52.

289. Kate Richards O'Hare, *Crime and Criminals,* originally published in 1929. Reprinted in *Prison Writings in 20th Century America,* edited by H. Bruce Franklin, (Middlesex, England: Penguin Books, 1998), 75.

290. Liz Benecchi, "Recidivism Imprisons American Progress," *Harvard Political Review,* August 8, 2021.

291. Gloria Anzaldúa, *Borderlands: La Frontera* (San Francisco, CA: Aunt Lute Books, 2007), 19. In the preface to the second edition, Anzaldúa describes "the Borderlands are physically present wherever two or more cultures edge each other, where people of different races occupy the same territory, where, under lower, middle and upper-class touch, where the space between two individuals shrinks with intimacy."

292. Ronnie Stephens, "Annual Prison Costs a Huge Part of State and Federal Budgets," *Interrogating Justice,* February 16, 2021. See also, Beatrix Lockwood and Nicole Lewis, "The Hidden Cost of Incarceration," *The Marshall Project,* December 17, 2019). See also "Price of Prison Spending in 2015," by *VERA.*

293. Statistics from US Department of Justice: Bureau of Justice Statistics. Compiled in Tara O'Neil Hayes, "The Economic Costs of the US Criminal Justice System," *American Action Forum,* July 16, 2020.

294. US Department of Justice, Bureau of Justice Statistics, "Recidivism and Reentry" page, updated regularly.

295. Liz Benecchi, "Recidivism Imprisons American Progress," *Harvard Political Review,* August 8, 2021.

296. Benjamin Boyce, *Dr. Junkie: One Man's Story of Addiction and Crime that will Challenge Everything you Know about the War on Drugs* (Baltimore, MA: Apprentice House, 2022).

297. Tupac Shakur, "Interview with Tanya Hart," (Six CINQ, 1992), YouTube.

Index

Acknowledgements

I was released from prison in 2005, but it didn't take long for me to get back into trouble. I didn't know what else to do. It was difficult to get a job doing anything other than minimum wage labor, and my support network of family and friends wasn't sure what to expect from me. To be honest, I wasn't sure what to expect from myself. I had begrudgingly accepted the felon label—Alexander's New Jim Crow—and that meant preparing for a life of subjugation and second-class status. My career options shrunk; I'd never be a cop, a lawyer, a service member, or an elected official. The requirement to confess things I had done on the worst days of my life to prospective employers, friends, relatives, and mentors showed up as the elephant in every room. My self-confidence and identity were reshaped in ways I only began to recognize decades later.

Meanwhile life went on, and that meant I had to do something every day. During one of my early meetings with my parole officer, he mentioned a parole requirement to maintain full time work, and then he added, "or full-time school." One of my biggest triggers for problematic drug use has always been mundane, drawn-out labor, the only work I could get as a parolee. On a whim, I filled out financial aid paperwork and applied to a couple Universities. And surprisingly, one of those schools accepted me: The University of Missouri in Kansas City, where I would earn my bachelor's degree.

The first few years were a clash of identities. I was terrified those in the Ivory Tower would discover my secret stain of criminality. Given my lengthy record, I didn't know what a degree would do for me even if I did manage to complete the program.

And I was still stuck in the mire of identity I had picked up in prison—the angry outlaw destined to reoffend until death. But as weeks became semesters became years became degrees, that identity evolved. It didn't go away, but it received a massive overhaul that fitted it with tools and knowledge for success. By the time I graduated from my bachelor's program, I knew I wanted to keep going. Thanks to the few people at UMKC who helped me hang in there until I got my feet beneath me.

There are so many people along the way who made this work possible, but a few stand out as vital to my success.

Dr. Stephen Hartnett was one of the first people to recognize my potential, and to spend time helping me edit my early rants and essays about crime and prison. His assistance in composing and editing this book was invaluable; it certainly wouldn't exist without him. He is also the person who hired me to teach college classes inside Colorado prisons, and his mentorship has been a guiding force in my post-incarceration journey. It's funny how you seldom realize how much people impact your journey in life until years later, when you look back and realize how far off the original path you've gone. It's been an incredible ride. Stephen Hartnett also heads up the annual publication of *Captured Words/Free Thoughts*, which features poetry, prose, artwork and academia from inside US prisons. Thanks to Stephen for, among other things, slightly reducing my cynicism.

Dr. Lisa Keränen assigned a chapter by an edgy art critic named Dave Hickey during one of my early master's degree seminars, and in so doing, she taught me that academic work doesn't have to be boring or stuffy. Lisa was also a committee member for my master's thesis, the project that provided the original notes for this book. And along the way she has fought with and for me as I struggled to get hired as a teacher even after I finished my PhD. Thanks to Dr.

K. for fighting to get me in the door. We talked about her work on episode 72 of my podcast, *The Dr. Junkie Show*.

It is not an exaggeration to say that Dr. Christian Foust kept me going through my PhD during those times when I nearly quit because it looked like I was permanently unemployable. She got me hired as a teacher, she found funding for my PhD classes when I was broke, and she has become a good friend and a treasured mentor. Her acceptance has been as valuable as her sincerity.

Dr. Bill Yousman got me thinking about prison films and public perception years ago with his article "Inside Oz: Hyperviolence, Race and Class Nightmares, and the Engrossing Spectacle of Terror." He has been incredibly supportive of my work along the way, and he was one of the first guests on my podcast, *The Dr. Junkie Show*, where we talked about his work on prison media in episode 32. Thanks to Bill for the vote of confidence, and for reading around my typos.

Finally, thanks to my students inside prison. I've never had a group of undergraduates hungrier to learn and more willing to engage than when I head behind the walls of Colorado's largest and oldest prisons (Sterling Correctional Facility and Territorial Correctional Facility, respectively). It's been quite a ride from prisoner to PhD, then on to college educator, but I'm certain I won't be the only person in those classrooms who successfully makes it. Keep up the good work!

About the Author

Benjamin Boyce, PhD. is a prison educator, an activist and an author. He currently hosts *The Dr. Junkie Show*, a podcast devoted to ending the war on drugs and embracing a harm reduction perspective focused on returning drug users to positions of social connection: jobs, organizations, family, friends, school, etc. During his early 20s, Dr. Boyce spent time locked up in the largest walled prison on Earth, in Jackson, Michigan. He currently teaches college classes both on campus and inside multiple Colorado prisons.

Reach out to Benjamin at Benjamin.Boyce@ucdenver.edu.

Find the podcast wherever you stream.

Apprentice
House Press
Loyola University Maryland

Apprentice House is the country's only campus-based, student-staffed book publishing company. Directed by professors and industry professionals, it is a nonprofit activity of the Communication Department at Loyola University Maryland.

Using state-of-the-art technology and an experiential learning model of education, Apprentice House publishes books in untraditional ways. This dual responsibility as publishers and educators creates an unprecedented collaborative environment among faculty and students, while teaching tomorrow's editors, designers, and marketers.

Eclectic and provocative, Apprentice House titles intend to entertain as well as spark dialogue on a variety of topics. Financial contributions to sustain the press's work are welcomed. Contributions are tax deductible to the fullest extent allowed by the IRS.

To learn more about Apprentice House books or to obtain submission guidelines, please visit www.apprenticehouse.com.

Apprentice House
Communication Department
Loyola University Maryland
4501 N. Charles Street
Baltimore, MD 21210
410-617-5265
info@apprenticehouse.com
www.apprenticehouse.com

CPSIA information can be obtained
at www.ICGtesting.com
Printed in the USA
LVHW040735290323
742860LV00012B/156